Uneasy City

UNEASY CITY

An Insider's View of the
City of London

FRANK WELSH

Weidenfeld & Nicolson · London

First published in Great Britain in 1986 by
George Weidenfeld & Nicolson Limited
91 Clapham High Street, London SW4 7TA

ISBN 0 297 78994 5

Printed by Butler & Tanner Ltd
Frome and London

Contents

CONTENTS

Tables

Acknowledgements

So many of those who have contributed to this book have asked that their names should not be mentioned that it would seem invidious to name any. At the same time it would be ungrateful not to thank Ken Robinson, Hugh Jones, Peter Hill, Tony Barnes and Dennis Weatherstone for their kindness.

The staff of Lloyd's, the Bank of England, the Securities Exchange Commission, the Institute of Bankers, the London & New York Stock Exchanges, the Securities & Investment Board, and the Cambridge University Appointments Board were invariably courteous and helpful. Anne Engel's patience was exemplary, and the industrious assistance of Benjamin, John and Agnes W, and of CATS, proved essential.

FRW

Note

With some reluctance, American billions – one thousand millions – are used throughout.

PART ONE

Ichabod

I

Vanishing London

'Where has commerce such a mart,
So rich, so thronged, so drained and so supplied
As London, opulent, enlarged, and still
Increasing London?'

WILLIAM COWPER

It is entirely understandable that many people, on hearing of the latest City scandal of absconding Lloyd's underwriters, of fraudulent share dealings, or of twenty-three-year-olds being paid – let us not say earning – hundreds of thousands of pounds a year, tend to insist, in some exasperation, that the law should take a firm grip of those manifestations of opulence and greed.

Responding with injured indignation the City will claim that the services it provides bring hundreds of millions into the economy, that the financial services industry is now the largest in the country, and that those involved should be left alone to sort out their own problems.

There is truth in both these attitudes, and this book is an attempt (based on more than twenty years' experience in bank boardrooms) to come as near veracity as possible. It represents a restricted and partial view; the commodity markets, the functions of large institutional investors, the mechanics of foreign exchange, the operations of the Baltic Exchange, and the governance of the City itself are touched on only tangentially. The text is necessarily restricted in that no insider, with detailed knowledge of one or two aspects of the City, can hope to be expert on every part of that complex entity; and partial in that so long a time spent in banking parlours and boardrooms induce many of a banker's prejudices.

There are some counterbalancing advantages. An informed outsider may present a more balanced synopsis, but must do so without the benefit of firsthand experience in making credit judgements, negotiating international loans, arguing with regulators, fighting protracted takeovers, conducting midnight telex discussions with the other side of the world, sniffing out frauds and agonizing over dubious debts, that is the normal lot of a working banker.

3

A brief explanation of my own experience will clarify matters. I joined William Brandt's Sons & Company Ltd in 1965, after ten years in commerce and industry, became successively a general manager and a managing director, and after the complete acquisition by National and Grindlays Bank remained a member of that board until its assimilation by the Australia and New Zealand Bank in 1985.

Brandt's was a venerable family-owned bank, the third most senior of the accepting houses, founded in London in 1805. Grindlays was a British overseas bank, with headquarters in London but having most of its business in the old imperial territories of the Indian subcontinent and East Africa, and later also in the Middle and Far East. Both banks have now disappeared as independent organizations.

At the same time I was able to pursue my own interest in industry, and founded the first venture capital organization within a British bank, as well as serving on the boards of a number of companies in many sectors of industry, on the Royal Commission on the National Health Service, the British Waterways Board, and other public enterprises.

As an adviser to the Lissauer Group I participated in their acquisition of a controlling interest in Henry Ansbacher, a small authorized bank, and sat on their board for a number of years. I have been an underwriting member of Lloyd's since 1974 and was on the board of Grindlay Brandt's Insurance until its acquisition by Citicorp.

The experiences were varied: collecting debts in the West African bush, investigating tourist potential in Afghanistan, establishing a toehold in Australia, building steelworks in Sheffield and Gateshead, evaluating North Sea oil ventures, and assisting in the purchase of Argentinian department stores. Some of the stormiest passages turned out to be the most instructive; in banking and insurance one learns, often quite sharply, from errors, especially one's own; when Brandt's was bought out by Grindlays many of the existing directors, believing (not incorrectly) the new policies to be dangerous, either resigned or were kicked upstairs to the parent company board. As chairman of Dunford and Elliot I led both aggressive and defensive bids, appeared before the Takeover Panel (and my admiration for the organization should be seen in the context of their having agreed with me!) and as a member of credit committees in three banks agreed with decisions which afterwards proved to be wrong.

There are unusually cogent reasons for addressing the subject of the City at the present time. The Bank of England, the Lord Mayor's procession, the Great Fire, Mansion House banquets, the Lutine Bell, turtle soup and fair round bellies and all, the City is part of national mythology, and like all myths, susceptible to a variety of explanations. But it is also an increasingly important national asset, and one currently exposed to rapid changes which are accompanied by both great opportunities and perils.

It is therefore essential to separate myth from reality in order to get things right at a time when getting things wrong could be very damaging. To render this task more complex, a good deal of deliberate obfuscation has been created. Dr Pangloss lives and thrives in EC 2; self-criticism is little practised, and the enthusiasm for keeping things as they are is proof against repeated near disasters.

The rest of the country is less sanguine. Many industrialists, politically sympathetic with City folk, are fiercely critical of what they believe to be superior and unhelpful attitudes to industrial problems: and frankly envious of the profits that are made there with apparent ease. Many of those politically opposed find the City too convenient a stalking horse to make an effort to comprehend how it works, and to weigh impartially its merits and defects, much preferring to strike out wildly at what they conceive to be capitalist iniquity.

As in any sharp contention facts are the first casualty. In spite of claims of industrial prosperity sometimes made by politicians, British manufacturing industry is declining, not only in comparison with international competition, but absolutely. Claims to the contrary may be feebly buttressed by the use of selective statistics, so here are a few incontrovertible facts from the British Institute of Management. Between 1971 and 1985 two and a half million jobs in manufacturing have been lost; manufacturing now represents 21 per cent of the total national output. Comparative proportions for other industrial countries are: Germany 31.8, Japan 30.55, France 25.3. The contribution of manufacturing to the UK balance of payments, which moved from £1,974 million to £5,066 million between 1974 and 1978, declined to a deficit of £3,785 million in 1984. Table No. 1, which is drawn from overseas trade statistics, published by HMSO, and shown in the NatWest quarterly review of February 1986, illustrates a dramatic deterioration in the balance of trade. While so steep a fall is unlikely to continue, only the most optimistic believe in the prospect of an enduring reversal.

Tacitly or openly acknowledging the accuracy of these unfortunate facts, the City emphasizes its own contrasting success. Sir Kenneth Berrill, chairman of the Securities and Investment Board (SIB), the new City regulatory authority, is passionate in his insistence on the need to ensure the success of an industry now more important than coal, steel and agriculture put together.

The City's claim to be the largest surviving industry is unfortunately accurate, but the suggestion sometimes made that services might replace lost manufacturing industry is not. In spite of the admitted real and substantial growth in financial services the relative importance of London

Table 1 Balance of UK trade

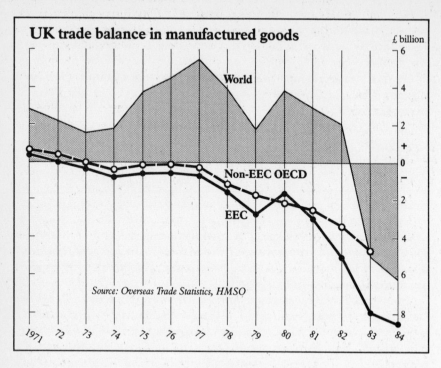

UK trade balance in manufactured goods
£ billion

World

Non-EEC OECD

EEC

Source: Overseas Trade Statistics, HMSO

1971 72 73 74 75 76 77 78 79 80 81 82 83 84

as a financial centre has actually slightly declined between 1979 and 1985, while that of New York has greatly increased.

A question, perhaps the most important economic question confronting Britain, is how long can London retain its share? The continuing success

Table 2 International financial market share

	December 1979 %	June 1985 %
UK	22.9	22.6
US	10.9	18.4
Other Europe	39.4	27.5
Offshore	21.1	23.3

(percentage of external claims of banks in domestic and foreign currency, Barclays Review, February 1986)

of the USA is connected with the liberalization of controls experienced there under the Reagan administrations. The City insists that minimum restrictions should be imposed if we are to match this: the government is concerned to protect the public; and the public is only patchily aware of the problem.

On the academic left the misconceptions are, perhaps knowingly, absurd. Richard Minns in his book '*Take Over the City*', published in 1982, exemplified this.

> How can the City be called 'powerful'? It does not actually make anything which can be of use to people or which can be sold at a profit. Instead, it offers money at a price to companies or individuals who want to make things. The City depends on companies and individuals wanting to produce for it to lend money.

Arguments based on so transparently inaccurate analyses cannot be other than fallacious, but since those who are ignorant of their history are doomed to repeat it, and nowhere more so than in the realm of economics, it is worth while beginning with a look at recent changes in what is called, for convenience, the City.

The City of London is more than a geographic expression; it remains the repository of an unmatched diversity of financial and commercial services. Its very diversity makes it unlikely that there should be truly a 'City opinion': stockbrokers, underwriters, bankers and commodity traders have different backgrounds, interests, and cultures. The temptation is always to claim that 'City opinion' reinforces one's own judgements. I have nevertheless found it impossible to avoid reference to the City as though it were an integrated entity and ask that this usage might be accepted with appropriate reservations.

Britain has successfully, if occasionally narrowly, avoided revolutionary change in modern times. A penalty for this success has been that evolutionary movements have progressed, often penetrating deeply, without being detected by those in positions of power, who have therefore been unprepared when some event enforced a confrontation. Progress – technological, philosophical and social – during the late eighteenth century had bypassed political institutions, the Law, the Crown, the churches, and the universities to an extent that brought a rude awakening when, at the end of the Napoleonic wars, it became apparent that the nation was out of tune with its institutions. Revolution was avoided only by fundamental and often precipitous changes in the fabric of society which altered irrevocably every facet of life in the ten years between 1820 and 1830 in a flurry of reform.

Britain in 1820 looked back either nostalgically or with abhorrence to

7

the eighteenth century: by 1850 it was transformed into an industrial and technological society, the workshop of the world not only in matters of industry but in the development of social and political ideas. The alteration took place with confusing speed; Lord Eldon, who defended such practices as the public hanging of a seven-year-old girl, was a contemporary of Lord Brougham, the originator of the study of social sciences.

The end of the Second World War brought about the same sort of situation. Industrial decline, together with technical advances, social expectations, and the fragmentation of Empire, forced themselves upon public attention. Attitudes towards changes remain today as dissimilar as those of Eldon and Brougham: the executioners and the optimists continue the same debate in only slightly different terms.

The extent of the change is by now clear: from being a great power, the centre of an empire and the most prosperous nation in Europe, we have become a dubiously second-rate country, with living standards now surpassed even by those in Italy, with traditional manufacturing industries in irretrievable ruin and a substantial proportion of the population violently disaffected. Universities and schools are closing, cities are becoming abandoned and derelict, and a sense of decay is almost palpable.

Institutions have adapted to circumstances with varying degrees of success. Naturally enough, it is in the most conservative areas of society that adaptation to change is seen to be most difficult and painful. The monarchy, the armed services, and even the churches have evolved to match altered conditions, but some bastions of inflexibility have remained solidly entrenched. Of these the trade unions and the City of London may be singled out as prime examples. It is hardly a coincidence that outside regulation of both financial institutions and trade unions have engendered the most passionate debates of recent years.

The City has proved more adaptable than the unions, a task, it might be thought, not too difficult of achievement. Only a very few years ago – twenty, let us say – the accepted picture of the City was of an area where Lutyens office blocks and the remains of Wren churches stood surrounded by bombed sites, populated by gentlemen in sedately cut, dark suits and white shirts with stiff collars, who always carried an umbrella and gloves; bowler hats were not obligatory, but recommended. Merchant bankers, who were pleased to be so called, had not yet degenerated into avaricious sharpness, and passed their days in parlours, warmed by coal fires, nourished on good sherry and bad luncheons, and addressed by deferential staff as 'Mr Evelyn', 'Mr Walter': heads of department (never, ever, referred to as 'bankers', a term reserved for a partner or director) were generally 'Mr Jones', although in moments of conviviality might be addressed as 'Jones'.

Clearing banks, undisturbed since their amalgamations at the end of the First World War, pursued the even tenor of their ways, protected by agreement not to compete for each other's customers, and always to keep their charges identical. Every manager had joined as a schoolboy and confidently expected to remain until his retirement, in whatsoever station it might please the board to call him.

Eastern Exchange bank officers, lean, bronzed men from the farther corners of the Empire, called in for chota pegs at the Falstaff at 11 a.m. sharp. They were the first to conclude the business of the day, but no one did much after one, at which hour the City collectively gave itself over to luncheon and the recovery therefrom.

The activities of bankers, if that is not too strong a word (banking is a watchful, but not, as Bagehot rightly said, a laborious trade) were supervised ('controlled' is altogether too forceful, and even 'supervised' suggests a consistency of monitoring that was not always the case: 'observed' might be more apt) by the Bank of England, concealing the iron hand of statutory power under the glove of what was charmingly called 'moral suasion', when someone looked like stepping out of line.

It was generally a homogeneous society: Paul Ferris, writing in 1960, commented:

> anyone without their background is immediately aware how similar they seem – no doubt he exaggerates the similarity, but the long easy vowels and the commanding style of speech do provide a uniform stamp. There is also the manner: a little casual, a little amateurish, never taking things too seriously . . .

Uniformity was apparent in the appearance of City men. Stiff collars were essential for the junior and middle ranks; starched cotton for executives, disposable paper for the unconventional indigent, and washable celluloid for the traditionalists. Directors could be allowed to wear white, or even cream, soft silk shirts, but one could go too far. Harald Peake, chairman of Lloyds Bank, was much criticized for wearing black suede shoes.

Revolutionary disturbance of the serene order of things had been safeguarded, since the Gordon riots of the eighteenth century, by the Bank piquet, a detachment of the Brigade of Guards, which was marched every evening from Wellington barracks to the Bank of England, much to the delight of tourists, under the command of a subaltern, who was given a very decent dinner by the Bank, a facility much appreciated by national servicemen.

Within the City a clearly defined system of rank was observed. The Bank of England, the Old Lady of Threadneedle Street, was unquestioned and supreme. Her equerries, the discount houses and the government

9

broker, shared her distinction, at least socially, for intellectually the accepting houses, the senior merchant banks, were considerably more elevated. There were a number of foreign banks, mainly European, but with Americans beginning to show an interest, all confining themselves very properly to the concerns of their countrymen and to their own nation's trade, as British banks centred their interests on what was known as the sterling area. Clearing banks were important, respectable, but dull; overseas banks rather raffish and picturesque.

Within the accepting houses two hierarchies were recognized; that of seniority which was immutable, according to the date of the firm's foundation in London – Barings, Rothschilds, Brandt's and the rest, and that of reputation, which was more changeable. Hambros were having a bad patch, and Lazards was not what it was; Philip Hill was expanding rapidly, and that man Warburg was making himself felt.

Outside banking circles Lloyd's could still be described as having 'a whiff of Boodle's about it' (McRae and Cairncross), and remained a community of some five thousand where everyone knew, or at least knew of, their fellows. Although Lloyd's itself was an institution of great distinction, some of which attached itself to the members, the business written there was declining as a percentage of total UK premium income, and the corporation was beginning to look like 'a duck-billed platypus – a creature whose unique form hardly justifies its successful survival' (McRae and Cairncross).

The bullion markets enjoyed a similar cachet. London was the centre from which the Bank of England, on behalf of the world's central banks, operated the gold pool and the market on which gold and silver were sold. Base metals were less glamorous, but almost as exclusive, with ring members rigorously screened and restricted in number by the committee of the London Metal Exchange; even New York followed the copper, lead, zinc and tin prices set in London. In much the same way the soft commodity dealers' associations operating as independent baronies continued to dominate the worlds' markets in coffee, cocoa, and tea, although jute, that mainstay of Dundee's industries, was already in terminal decline.

Those in positions of power within the banks continued to come almost invariably from a very similar background. It was rare to find a bank chairman or even an outside director who had not been to a major public school (half the chairmen of the accepting houses had been to Eton) and to Oxford or Cambridge (but general managers and executive directors, equally usually, had not, and sat below the salt).

When it was revealed at the Bank Rate Tribunal of 1959, an enquiry which gave a rare glimpse into the inner workings of the City, that conversations in which the Governor of the Bank of England had participated took place on a grouse moor, popular sentiment was gratified. Bankers were seen to be behaving in the way that had always been expected of them.

Even reprobates were expected to conform to the current mores. When Sir Denys Colquhoun Flowerdew Lowson, Bt (Winchester and Christ Church, Lord Mayor of London, Church Commissioner, Officer of the Orders of Orange Nassau, St Olaf, the Dannebrog, etc., and a member of the MCC), was exposed as having made £5 million by selling assets to a public company under his control for more than they had cost he defended his action as 'fair and reasonable' and described the enforced restitution he made as 'in accordance with the best interests of the City of London'.

Allowing for any exuberant exaggeration this is a not inaccurate picture of the City a quarter of a century ago; it is most decidedly not that of the City today. Since then we have seen three attempts to ensure the control of banking activities – the Competition and Credit Control Policy of 1971, the Banking Act of 1979, and the 1985 White Paper on banking and finance. The greatest financial crisis since the 1930s, as one governor put it, has been weathered, but another threatens on the international scene. Takeovers and mergers have reached unprecedented size and heights of acrimony, straining the regulatory bodies beyond credibility. The London Metal Exchange has failed to prevent the collapse of the tin market. New securities markets have burgeoned, as well as old frauds. New groupings are uniting very different financial operations and cultural traditions. Lloyd's has (it very much hopes) reformed itself, and the rest of the City is evolving a system of central controls, amid some nervousness as to their likely efficacy.

Although it may not yet be popularly accepted, attitudes have altered radically in the last twenty-five years; the City is no longer entirely a preserve of the upper middle classes; hypocrisy does not remain fashionable; the pursuit of profit appears paramount; traditional ordered patterns are kaleidoscoping. How permanent and real these changes may be is by no means so clear, nor what might be the eventual resolutions of current hyperactivity, but amid the flux one institution remains proverbial for reliability and solidity, the Old Lady of Threadneedle Street.

2

The Norman Conquest

'The Bank . . . is one of the best establishments, that
ever was made for the good of the Kingdom.'

MICHAEL GODFREY 1696

The City's tone is set by the Bank of England, and the Bank of England
in the 1960s was still, twenty years after his retirement, the child of that
remarkable man Montagu Norman, Governor of the Bank of England
for an unparalleled quarter-century, from 1920 to 1944. Both Norman's
grandfathers had been Governors, and he served in both the family banks,
Martins and Brown Shipley, as well as picking up a DSO in the Boer War,
before joining the Bank of England in 1915. During an eventful period of
office he established the authority of the Bank as the lender of last resort,
with a responsibility not only to the banking community but to the nation
as a whole. In the words of his biographer, Sir Henry Clay,

> He completed the transition of the Bank from commercial to central
> banking, reorganized it, and established its authority; London, although
> affected by every economic dislocation in the world, was never shaken
> by bank failure. He widened the conception of his responsibilities – from
> the money market to industry, from the United Kingdom to Europe
> and the Empire; if no one else would take a credit risk necessary to save
> a Government from collapse or a firm of national importance from
> bankruptcy he would take it. His approach to his problems was empiri-
> cal, seldom doctrinaire. He resisted the extension of government inter-
> vention in business affairs, because he feared that economic issues would
> be settled on irrelevant political grounds, or that government action
> would be too slow.

This distrust of government intervention, more impolitely known as interference, which subsequent events have done nothing to diminish, is still
the predominant sentiment in the City, and lies behind the current ten-
acious effort to have the City's affairs settled internally among the practitioners themselves. Conscious of successive governments' handling of
commercial matters, and contemplating the ruins of British shipbuilding,

12

the Land Rover and Westland incidents, it is not difficult to agree with the demand of self-government.

The Bank of England did not succeed to its present position as the guide and conscience of the City immediately or without protest from other sources. The crisis year is usually said to be 1890, when the great house of Baring, a more important institution then than now, was only saved from collapse by the action of the Bank of England in bullying and cajoling other banks into offering their support. Barings survived, and remains as the most traditional and one of the pleasantest of merchant banks; but one of the senior partners at Brandt's observed to me, as I set off to luncheon there in 1968, that Barings had 'never been quite the same since that nasty business of theirs, but were quite sound again now'.

The First World War brought a further crop of troubles for the Bank's attention. Cox and Kings, a company of which I was for some time Chairman, although not particularly large, were Army agents, and had a number of influential customers. When they landed in trouble Lloyds Bank was persuaded to buy the firm out, the expense being underwritten by the Bank of England at an eventual cost of £250,000. From that date on there was little doubt but that the Bank of England under Montagu Norman would arrange some sort of support for any British bank that found itself in difficulties. In 1928 Williams Deacon's, the Manchester bank, came to the end of its tether, stretched by loans to the cotton industry; it had made use of the device, still available to some banks, of not disclosing reserves, and had been transferring sums from these to profit for several years, in order to give the appearance, which in fact was illusory, of continuing profitability. The collapse of the cotton industry made it impossible to continue with this course, and the Royal Bank of Scotland was persuaded, not unwillingly, to buy out the Lancashire bank. True to banking traditions of confidentiality there was no intention of admitting the true state of affairs to shareholders, and therefore to the public at large; the matter was dealt with in the most discreet manner, but at a cost to the Bank of England of over £3 million, an enormous sum at that time.

Even the small and badly-managed firm of Frederick Hoth was the subject of a rescue; the failure of Hoth would certainly have caused no great upheaval, but the senior partner also happened to be a director of the Bank of England. Objections were raised, but Norman was prepared to put his foot down: 'In the interests of the banking and commercial community, Hoth must not be allowed to fail. In order to enable them to continue some arrangement to assist them must be made without delay.' The signal was as clear as in the rescue of Johnson Matthey Bankers fifty years later; the reputation of the London market must come first and the Bank would take responsibility for ensuring its preservation.

Montagu Norman went further than many subsequent governors have
felt able to do, and accepted responsibility for assisting manufacturing
industry, then regarded as being of prime importance to the prosperity of
the nation. When the great slump and depression came the Bank was
active. Armstrong Whitworth of Newcastle was admittedly a customer of
the Bank of England's Newcastle branch, but when it encountered liquidity
problems the Bank went far beyond the requirements of normal banking
practice. Not only were the company's credit lines extended, but the
Bank took the leading role in securing Armstrong's future, appointing a
'company doctor' in a reorganization that culminated in the merger of the
armaments side of Armstrong Whitworth with Vickers, creating the famous
company of Vickers-Armstrong.

The fashion in which the Bank of England exercises its by now unquestioned authority in the City derives from Norman's own character. He
had two basic principles; that the City should be allowed to go about its
own business free from interference by politicians or civil servants, who
had no concept of the way in which business affairs were conducted, and
that all arrangements were best made as quietly and privately as might
be between the fewest possible number of people. The first is still as valid
as ever; politicians of no party have shown any disposition to forgo what
is seen as electoral advantage in the pursuit of stability. The latter, as the
benefits of openness become more appreciated, is unfortunate. Norman
was himself a man little suited to public debate and given to operating on
a personal basis. The City has only recently begun to shed the habits of
secrecy that Norman encouraged.

Nationalization, which came shortly after Norman's retirement, only
extended the powers of the bank, and was carried out with a minimal
political fuss; Sir John Anderson, in the course of the debate in the
House of Commons, objected that 'in response to some ideological urge
a relationship moulded by long tradition is being replaced by formal
enactment', but the Bank itself, then under the firm hand of Lord Catto,
was relaxed. Hugh Dalton was able to record at the time that 'it was
with the Governor of the Bank that I had a constant and confidential
relationship' and the nationalization 'was one of our peaceful revolutions.
It has gone through wonderfully easily.' Nor, somewhat surprisingly, has
there since been a call to 'privatize' the Bank of England.

The Treasury was authorized by the 1946 Nationalization Act to give
directions to the Bank (but only after consulting the Governor), and the
Bank was for the first time given statutory powers to direct the affairs of
commercial banks. 'The Bank, if they think it necessary in the public
interest, may request information from and make recommendations to
bankers, and may, if so authorized by the Treasury, issue directions to any

bankers.' Although at first perturbed about this extension of regulatory powers banks have in practice since been willing to take what the Old Lady herself asks as a command, especially perhaps since the tradition of doing so very politely continued, in the Norman tradition of 'moral suasion'.

These powers, which in fact are greater than those of most other central banks, have been widely if discreetly used. The Bank may compel banks to observe capital ratios, to hold reserves with itself, to alter charges, to favour one class of borrower rather than another, and may control much of the detail of a bank's activities. In discussing problems of statutory regulation and self-regulation it is important to acknowledge that the success of the Bank of England in assuring the continuity of business is ultimately dependent upon statutory powers that the historian of banking, R. S. Sayers, describes as 'unparalleled elsewhere'.

And in spite of secondary banking and Johnson Matthey scandals the Bank of England has been strikingly successful in its supervisory role.

For generations no respectable British bank has been allowed to fail. Every crisis has been dealt with by negotiation as it has arisen, and the situation recovered. Contrast this, opponents of statutory regulation may claim, with the state of things in the USA, where, in spite of a massive structure of Federal regulatory authority in place for over seventy years, American banks continue to fail, and fail in considerable numbers. In the three years 1982–5 one hundred and sixty-nine US banks failed.

The happy state of things in Britain was not due entirely to the skills of the Bank of England, nor its statutory powers, but owed much to the static condition of British banking. The thirty years between 1890 and 1920 saw the multitude of country banks coalesce into five clearing banks, all centred in London within a few hundred yards of each other, which between them handled most of the domestic banking business. No new banks were founded although some of the smaller institutions were able to retain their independence. Problems of licensing and registration did not arise, and communications were as convenient as they could be.

Nor were the signs after the Second World War such as to indicate the prospect of radical change. The City of London, its physical structure shattered by German bombs, seemed fated to participate in the national decline; foreign investment had been lost or expended in the war effort; the Empire was moving towards inevitable dissolution; manufacturing industry, worn by the demands of conflict, looked in vain for regeneration. A decline duly occurred. Sterling itself lurched from crisis to crisis in spite of the cumbersome wartime regulations that persisted, like rationing, long after the emergency was ended, and ceded its place as a reserved currency to the dollar. For some time after 1948 the Bretton Woods agreement helped to postpone the worst consequences, but at the cost of storing up troubles against the inevitable dissolution of that compact.

The stage appeared set for banking to accompany all those other props of the economy on the gradual slide to oblivion – together with the shipbuilding industry, the merchant marine, steel-making, motor manufacture, textiles, and machine tools, to join the great departed. There are some useful lessons in why it did not do so, but rather survived and flourished.

The pre-war City had been part of that enormous, and largely still unrecognized, feat of social engineering that had made possible a century of British world power. A host of public schools, equipped with brand new traditions, turned out imperial officers and administrators; new orders of chivalry graded precisely according to seniority and social standing (as indeed they still are, and a very comical business it is!) were invented to reward them. The survival of these attitudes in society at large is perhaps not a matter of first-rate importance, but when they have affected relations in commerce and industry the result has been severely to damage competitive performance. First-class people have, until very recently, shied away from industry, preferring more socially acceptable careers in the professions, the foreign and home civil services and the arts. Manufacturing industry has suffered in consequence.

The more damaging effects were avoided in the City; banking, like brewing, was seen as a superior variety of trade, in which a gentleman might well engage. It was a career open to the talents; given the essential virtues of stamina, probity, and adaptability, emigrants started on an equal footing, and quickly succeeded. Lord Overstone, the great nineteenth-century Governor, wrote to Montagu Norman's father, then a Deputy Governor,

> I congratulate you on the strong infusion of the Jewish element into your bank's direction – I have before me a letter of Ricardo in which he expresses his astonishment that the Bank Directors with the opportunities before them had not accumulated much larger profits. I presume you do not mean any longer to expose yourself to his censure.

Fuelled by a rich mix of ability the City adapted creatively to the conditions of the nineteenth century. Lloyd's won the lion's share of all international insurance; the world's shipping contracts were placed on the Baltic Exchange; the finances of distant countries depended upon the prices obtained for their products on the London commodity exchanges. Merchant banks financed imperial communications, the infrastructure and industries of a number of foreign companies and arranged loans for governments. Clearing banks funded the massive sums involved in overseas trade, and British overseas banks provided safe and respectable services from Chittagong to Valparaiso.

Logically speaking, all this should have been expected to disappear along with solar topees and battleships; that it did not is as remarkable as it has been unremarked. The post-war City did not appear to be a powerful engine of change. There had been no new member of the Accepting Houses Committee since its establishment in 1914. Insurance, commodity and Stock Exchange firms and merchant banks were still largely family businesses, with only the clearing banks recruiting significantly from outside, and that only at the lowest levels.

The clearing banks looked set to continue their long period of inactivity, exemplars of stagnation, too large to fear competition except from each other, and avoiding this by means of a clearly defined cartel. Since 1918, when the Big Five were formed, 80 per cent of all banking business had been split between them. Lending practices had become ossified and uniform. Any display of orginality was discouraged; clearing bankers had to be agreeable to customers and to ensure that their securities were perfected. They were not expected to invent new ways of doing business.

In a country where schools, universities, law courts and Parliament all close in time for the hay harvest to be gathered in and reconvene only when the corn harvest has been garnered, and where the budget is produced for the spring sowing, it is perhaps invidious to blame the banking system for remaining wedded to concepts that have been outdated at least since the arrival of steam and the invention of the telegraph, but the clearing banks in the 1960s did seem quite remarkably resistant to change.

All innovations were equally frowned upon; clearing banks concentrated on the provision of overdrafts to industry and commerce, merchant and overseas banks on the finance of trade by negotiating bills. Both these methods of finance were intended to be short term; overdrafts were agreed for a single year, while bills had a tenor of 90 or 180 days, being the time it should take a sailing ship to complete its voyage. Neither system, as clearing-bank industrial customers frequently complained, was designed to provide long-term finance, which continental banks, founded specifically for this purpose and capitalized accordingly, could make available. British bankers were adamant: it was an article of faith that borrowing short and lending long must result in ruin, and since clearing banks were and are massively financed by that most volatile of sources – current account surpluses provided interest free by customers keeping their accounts in credit – lengthy loans must be shunned.

The limitations of accounting techniques – customers' accounts were often handwritten until the late 1950s, with only the simplest form of machinery then taking over – allowed branches to have a higher degree of independence than is now the practice, and managers enjoyed greater responsibility. Executor and Trustee business continued to be important, and branches were able to offer all the services most of their customers wanted, arranging their affairs and offering advice. Local general managements had, in turn, wide powers, and were expected to negotiate directly with even the largest companies in their area.

The quality of junior staff was high and entry competitive. Almost all recruits came straight from school, and this continued until very recently. Promotion was slow but tolerably certain for the able, provided they avoided either bad debts or dissolute habits.

Merchant banks, being much smaller (and it is rarely realized how small some highly regarded banks are), had more active boards, but even here there was sharp differentiation. Banking business – foreign exchange, money market, acceptances – tended to be handled by professionals, who were not directors, while foreign loans, company finance and portfolio management were dealt with by the directors, who generally had family connections.

The Bank of England did not find it difficult to supervise the activities of the banking clients, all of whom had the head office within a few minutes' walk. The chairmen of clearing banks were dealt with individually, the accepting houses through the Accepting Houses Committee, and the discount houses through the London Discount Market Association. Given half an hour's notice the Deputy Governor could have them all in his office for a chat.

The activities of all these banking institutions was shrouded in secrecy. Banks designated under section VII of the Companies Act 1947 – effectively all the well-established houses of whatever size – were allowed to hold undisclosed reserves, making it impossible to gauge the real strength or weakness of their balance sheets or their current profitability. Profits could be tucked away and losses made good without outsiders becoming any the wiser. There were conventions that reported profits ought in some way to reflect the real situation, but these had conventional status only. Barings chose for many years, with patrician equanimity, to report reserves only to an appropriate round million pounds.

The privilege was heatedly defended by banks as being necessary to preserve public confidence; interestingly enough the same argument is currently being advanced by banks reluctant to accede to the greater degree of disclosure being demanded by American authorities. Ill-informed comment, it is claimed – any comment critical of banks is considered by them either tasteless or ill-informed – might undermine the security of the whole financial system.

The appearance of complacent traditionalism was illusory. A ferment

18

was taking place in the 1960s which, while driving prudent banks to extraordinary errors of judgement and producing a succession of financial scandals unparalleled since the days of Hatry and Stavisky, has again established the City of London as the centre of international finance; at least for the moment.

The following chapters note some of the more important developments in the City during the last twenty years or so and the way in which these have led to the situation in 1986. The process of change is continuous, and any description outdated as soon as written, but an understanding of the forces that make for change is essential in any attempt to evaluate it or to forecast the future.

3

Wind of Change

'It is the great Advantage of a trading Nation that
there are few in it so dull and heavy, who may not
be placed in Stations of life which may give them an
Opportunity of making their Fortunes.'

ADDISON.

Effective reforms are often achieved by outsiders. When institutions have
decayed to the point of being held in general disrepute, unpleasant action
is needed, and a certain distancing from the subject makes this easier.

Mr Rupert Murdoch and Mr Ian MacGregor, for example, while
employing coarse and insensitive methods, have achieved permanent and
essential changes in their industries, which they might well have found
more difficult had they been brought up in this country and shared its
peculiar ethos.

Operating in a more civilized fashion but being even more of an outsider,
Siegmund Warburg, who came to England in 1934, changed the habits
and traditions of the City with equally decisive effect. As Montagu Norman
defined the way in which the Bank of England operates, Warburg set the
pattern which other merchant banks have since followed.

He was a member of an ancient and influential Sephardic Jewish
banking family, coming originally from Italy (where a forebear, one
Andrea Christian del Banco, was a money changer in Pisa), but settling
in the sixteenth century in the Westphalian town of Warburg from
which they then took their name. By the nineteenth century the house
of M. M. Warburg was a leading German bank: Siegmund's great-
grandfather was a deputy in the German parliament, whose sister Sarah
was a friend of both Heine and Bismarck. Sarah's grandson Max was asked
to lead the German financial delegation to the Versailles conference, but
by 1933 it was clear to Siegmund, if not to others of the family, that the
prospects in Germany were grim, and that London or New York must be
the centres of the future.

He chose London, much to London's good, and in 1934 established the
New Trading Company. This was no offshoot of his family bank, but
Siegmund's own creation, with a modest capital of £120,000 subscribed

20

as to 10 per cent by Siegmund, the other shareholders being Harry Lucas, Richard Jessel, the Berliner Handelsgesellschaft and the Dutch International Corporation. Not being a Warburg family bank the New Trading Company was, unlike any other merchant bank at that time, open to outsiders in the manner of the previous century. His first recruits comprised two Englishmen, Sir Lewis Sterling and K. L. Guinness, two Germans, E. G. Thallman and Henry Grunfeld, and an Austrian, Eric Korner. Henry Grunfeld was one of the ablest men the City had seen in recent times and, like Siegmund, fired by the ambition to prove himself in a new country.

The policy of recruiting the best and catching them young continued, and at a time when the senior positions in all other banks were family preserves, enabled Warburg's to scintillate. Since like attracts like, they continue to do so. In its first years the new company did little in the way of innovative business, until shortly after the outbreak of the Second World War. Realizing the importance of securing supplies, Siegmund put together in May 1940 a syndicate composed of three of the oldest accepting houses, Rothschilds, William Brandt's and Hambros, in order to provide finance for imports, especially from America. It proved rapidly successful, and represented Warburg's first significant international move.

After the war the New Trading Company was re-established as a conventional merchant bank, S. G. Warburg & Co., and began its traditions of prompt starting, impeccable documentation, a certain briskness and the worst food in the City. Profits rose steadily from £40,000 in 1945 to £200,000 in 1953, and in 1958 Warburgs were able to buy out Seligman Brothers, an original member of the Accepting Houses Committee. This was something of an opportunity, being the first time in more than fifty years that an Accepting House had come on the market. Warburg's celebrated their new status by initiating what came to be known in the City as the Great Aluminium War.

Company mergers were by no means new to the City: the big banks themselves were the product of generations of takeovers and acquisitions, as were such industrial giants as ICI, Unilever and Shell. But publicly disputed takeovers were; often enough mergers had been enforced by the virtual inability of the weaker party to survive – not unnaturally such processes were often accompanied by some acerbity, but this was kept hidden, at a gentlemanly level, undisclosed to the world at large.

There was no reason why, when the Reynolds Aluminium Company of America wished to acquire a stake in the British aluminium industry, the affair could not have been managed in the same way. A few tangential questions to interested parties, leading to a chat over tea in someone's club (a favourite rendezvous for business discussions of this sort, providing an excuse to be in the West End rather than the City at that time of day, secure from prying eyes) with the chairman, should have secured an agreement which would have kept the existing directors in the style they had become accustomed to. The accountants could have been left to sort out the detail.

This sort of operation was simply inconceivable to Siegmund when Reynolds, advised by Kuhn Loeb, asked Warburg's to proceed with the bid: he was not a man willing, or even able, to reach comfortable accommodations, and even today the house he founded is not noted for easy charm and graceful entertainment: it continues to rely, as he did, on a carefully prepared and logical case. The Reynold's/Tube Investment bid for British Aluminium therefore developed into a national event: the Aluminium War.

There is little merit in telling the story yet again; Joseph Wechsberg does so in his book *The Merchant Bankers*, an account upon which all subsequent treatments, including that of Jacques Attali, rely. The crux of the matter was that everything became public. Instead of civilized agreements over tea, a battle was fought in the public prints. Faced with a direct approach, the City Establishment interpreted it as an attack.

A vintage crop of hypocrisy was forthcoming. Lord Portal, chairman of British Aluminium, reproached for turning down out of hand an offer of 78/- a share, while toting the shares to a rival bidder for 60/-, and not breathing a word of this to his shareholders, responded stiffly that 'those familiar with negotiations between great companies will realize that such a course would have been impracticable'. Lord Kindersley invoked the national interest; another banker was quoted as claiming that British Aluminium must be saved for civilization.

Warburg attributed the venom to a dislike of him as 'a Jew, a newcomer, the sort who had not been to English schools and who spoke English with a foreign accent'. It was more than this; the City discerned in Warburg, to whom 'laziness and self-satisfaction' were the greatest sins, a mortal threat to its continuing comfortable existence.

Lord Portal produced a formidable defence team; to defeat the Reynolds bid fourteen out of the seventeen accepting houses were joined with the Governor of the Bank of England and the Prime Minister. Warburg, who had never thought much either of the Bank of England or the sort of gentlemanly conservatism represented by Harold Macmillan, was not put off. The press, and ultimately the shareholders, sided with him. Reynolds obtained control of British Aluminium.

It was not the first of disputed takeovers, for history is rarely so obligingly tidy, but it was the first to highlight the issues so starkly. The City was seen to be uniting to resist a reasonable, even a generous, offer, without any considered rationale and with no clear interests to defend, except perhaps those of the directors themselves, and objecting for no perceptibly sound reason except that the bid was made by outsiders muscling in. Once the facts were revealed to the public, however, the game was up, and Lord Portal lost his job, although the pill was sugared with a payment of £30,000, even at today's rates a reasonable golden handshake, and then a considerable sum indeed.

Jacques Attali describes the effect that the *coup de tonnerre* had in the City.

> From that time on it was no longer shameful to rise early and work hard. Discussion of financial matters was no longer confined to gentlemen's clubs, but took place in the market itself. No board, no privileged shareholder was henceforth safe from a *coup d'état*. All the venerable traditions and good name of the City were in pieces. For better and for worse.

The *Financial Times*, in Siegmund's obituary, commented of this episode that: 'he had been looked at by his opponents as a parvenu financier. This extraordinary perversion of reality illustrates the weakness of the Establishment at the close of the '50s and its isolation from the great international movements of the time'.

The Aluminium War began a springtide of takeover bids, which has continued, with ebbs and flows, ever since and has brought radical alterations to industrial attitudes. A number of the currently most important commercial and industrial groups are the product of a campaign of takeover battles, continued over many years by such master strategists as Charles Clore and Maxwell Joseph. Sears Holdings and Grand Metropolitan are both examples of successful serial bids: both groups tried in turn for Watneys, Maxwell Joseph eventually winning with what was, at the time, a record price.

Even the takeovers that never happened were influential, for the possibility of an unwelcome bid acted as a clear warning to potential victims that management must keep on its toes, and from the early 1960s new standards of professional industrial management were set. Nothing concentrates the mind of a board better than the suspicion that a predatory rival has them in their sights.

Takeovers and mergers lead to nervousness on the part of workers as well as directors: boards of taken-over companies are almost always, politely or otherwise, compensated or not, immediately or after a decent interval, shown the door; this they tend to dislike. Workers have much the same fear, although these are more equally shared by the workforces of both pursuers and pursued. In spite of whatever claims may be made mergers are almost always accompanied by rationalization, which is a synonym for job losses. In the long run these may be balanced by new employment opportunities made possible by expansion, but this long term, if it eventuates, tends to be very long indeed.

What research has been done on the results of mergers in the companies involved is inconclusive, and does not indicate at all clearly that any permanent benefits accrue. Indeed, it can be argued that they have served British industry badly, and the subsequent history of the British aluminium industry may be cited in this context. But it is also possible that the concentration on short-term performance that would enable a board either to have a premium rating attached to their shares, putting them either into an advantageous position to make a bid, or to defend themselves against one, has had quite serious effects on British industrial investment. (German businesses, to put it mildly, do not seem to perform perceptibly worse than their British counterparts, but do so without the benefit of that competition which is supposed to be stimulated by takeover bids. Mergers are carried out, usually with the assistance of banks who control strategic shares, with a gentlemanly reticence far removed from the razzmatazz of a British takeover fight.)

The case against publicly contested bids runs as follows. For historical reasons long-term bank finance has not been available to British companies, who have satisfied their capital requirements either from retained profits or from raising equity on the Stock Exchange. Whether for this or other reasons the level of investment in British industry has been consistently and significantly lower than in the economies of our competitors. The effects of underinvestment have been for some years cushioned by skills and equipment inherited from the days of our industrial hegemony, but these have now been dispersed.

Modern plant and equipment have grown more complex and expensive, and the time taken to bring new ventures to profitability has been extended. A simple machine shop, with tools bought off the shelf, and an existing, adequately trained, workforce, can be into profit almost immediately. A numerically controlled production line and associated product design will cost a great deal more and take longer to make any contribution; it will also employ a fraction of the number of workers.

Managements have been reluctant to incur the immediate expense and disruption in return for a delayed profitability, and therefore been tempted to hang on to out-of-date plant and replace it only when resources were available; one well-loved large machine tool in the Sheffield works of Hadfields had come from France before the Franco-Prussian war.

To make matters worse, access to new capital was rendered difficult to the point of impossibility over many years by the joint effects of the Labour

24

government's policy of dividend restrictions and high interest rates, the effects of which were predictable and damaging, but which were for unconvincing political reasons disregarded.

An investor puts out money in the hope of either dividends, a capital gain, or both. When interest rates are high handsome returns can be had from government securities without any risk, and therefore investment in equities is only made with a view to potential capital gains. If dividends are restricted, the share price of any company will only be able to move in accordance with general market fluctuations, or downwards should its own performance be poor. However well the company does the board may not increase the reward given to shareholders by way of dividend; any gain can therefore only be brought about in some other way. A takeover, made or received, can provide the answer; but job losses are the inevitable concomitant. In anything more than the shortest of runs a strategy of ambush is not the wisest way of ensuring industrial growth.

The problem was exacerbated by the Labour government's other policy of absurdly high tax rates on what was called 'unearned income', which at one time rose over 100 per cent, at a time when capital gains tax was at 30 per cent. Investment was therefore entirely directed at achieving capital gains, which could be done either by holding gilts to maturity (for government borrowing had to be protected) or by buying likely takeover subjects, emphasizing the casino-like operation of the Stock Exchange.

Thus long-term structural unemployment was caused to no small extent by the workers' party's own policies, a fact which was forcibly pointed out to them at the time by a number of us. Judging from the latest pronouncements it is not clear that this has yet been understood.

Whatever its economic results might be, the contested takeover bid became a conspicuous feature of the City scene, as merchant banks revived their company finance departments, which hitherto had been concerned only with the occasional flotation, introduction, rights issue or agreed merger, but were now expanded by recruiting accountants and lawyers. In the course of so doing they rechristened themselves, following an American fashion, as corporate finance departments.

The burgeoning takeover business caused problems, in one of the most significant of which my own bank, William Brandt's Sons & Co., became involved. It turned out to be both the prototype of many future battles and an instructive example of the City's failure to understand the realities of industrial existence.

4

The Pergamon Affair

'Saul Saul, wherefore persecutest thou me?'

SHAREHOLDER'S QUESTION AT THE PERGAMON LTD
EXTRAORDINARY GENERAL MEETING 1969

Robert Maxwell and Saul Steinberg have much in common: they are very able, self-made men, independent to the point of wilfulness, who have been and continue to be extremely successful, and with whom more sedate establishment figures find it difficult to deal.

When they first met it seemed that they at least understood each other, and when a merger was negotiated in 1969 between their two companies, Pergamon and Leasco, it was done by the principals meeting face to face in a hotel lobby without the presence of advisers. This proved to be an error; merchant bankers may be expensive but they have their uses, and are usually able to make deals stick together if that is what their principals really want. When exposed to professional scrutiny the proposed deal quickly fell apart at the seams. Robert Fleming & Co., who had been advising Pergamon, resigned. The intended allies became enemies and the remainder of the City establishment, sympathizing with the devil they didn't know rather than the one they did, chose to back Steinberg in an effort to unseat Maxwell. No other accepting house was prepared to take Fleming's place until William Brandt's, at the suggestion of the Bank of England, was asked to do so. Believing it to be quite wrong that a public company should not have proper advice, and with the backing of Lord Aldington, chairman of Grindlays, Brandt's parent company, the invitation was accepted. For the next five years Brandt's, in the person of their representative, Alastair Thomson, did their considerable best to keep Pergamon on the rails.

The operation afforded a rare view of the difficulties the City at that time had in comprehending how industry worked, and the tendentious hypocrisy of which some elements were capable. An Extraordinary General Meeting which packed the Connaught Rooms marked the beginning of an instructive episode. It had been called by the controlling institutional shareholders who had formed a committee headed by Norman Freeman,

26

of the ICI Pension Fund, for the specific purpose of unseating Maxwell from the chair and replacing his largely executive board with Leasco sympathizers. The committee, independently advised by Schroders, being firmly anti-Maxwell, the result of the meeting was expected to be a foregone conclusion.

Leasco, advised by Jacob Rothschild, suspected that Robert Maxwell would avoid the outcome of the meeting by some device, such as 'deciding overnight to hold it in Greenland and flying a plane-load of Maxwell supporters there', which was legally possible. Brandt's secured Maxwell's assurance that he would not do this, and passed it on to Rothschilds, who declined to accept the undertaking and obtained an injunction restraining him from any such action.

To anyone with the most superficial knowledge of human nature this was an error. Robert Maxwell is difficult, and can be overbearing and disingenuous, but as he had given his word, according to City convention the matter should have been regarded as settled; and if it was good enough for Brandt's it ought to have been good enough for Rothschilds.

The gloves were off. The meeting, which was handled by Maxwell with superb skill, showing his opponents in an uncomfortably awkward light, took place next day as planned. When a poll was taken the institutions voted as expected; Pergamon was given a new board, with Brandt's being asked to continue to act as their advisers even although their advice to the shareholders had been that Maxwell should be retained as essential to the future of their investment. The advice was not taken: Robert Maxwell was given his marching orders and a pillar of the establishment, Sir Henry d'Avigdor-Goldsmid, was appointed as chairman in his place. Both Schroders and Rothschilds also remained in their capacity as advisers to the institutional shareholders and Leasco respectively, while the board settled down to attempt the direction of Pergamon.

It speedily became apparent that Pergamon without Maxwell amounted to very little. The central and much the most profitable section of the company's business comprised the publication of learned journals bought by universities and libraries throughout the world. The editors and contributors of these made it clear that they were loyal Maxwell men, would negotiate only with him, and that without his co-operation the business would collapse: which was, of course, exactly what Brandt's had been saying. Sir Henry was fiercely opposed to Maxwell, with the antipathy for new men that always characterizes a settled establishment, but complicated by the jealousies that arose from the peculiar circumstances that Maxwell, who had started life in a remote Czechoslovak village, had fought his way into the British Army, earned a Military Cross, become a Member of Parliament, established a new industry and made a fortune, while Sir

Henry had inherited his title, wealth, and position from a family that had been settled in England since Cromwell's time.

A managing director was found by Leasco, who speedily proved unsuitable and had to be expensively disposed of, and Sir Henry, who found the whole business distressing, resigned in 1972 in favour of Sir Walter Coutts, chairman of one of Grindlay's associates.

Sir Walter, who as Governor-General of Uganda had been used to dealing with personages quite as awkward as Captain Maxwell, immediately grasped the nettle. He met the scientific editors in America and they, in his own words, 'made it absolutely clear to me, that if we did not put Bob Maxwell back, not only onto the Board, but as chairman and managing director of Pergamon, they would withdraw their support of Pergamon Press'. Due to the continuing hostility of the Freeman committee this proved impossible, but Maxwell accepted a compromise whereby he would take charge of publishing and marketing as 'non-executive' director of a subsidiary.

Three things were then quite clear to Brandt's: the prosperity of Pergamon depended upon Robert Maxwell, who was prepared to provide this for the benefit of the shareholders as a whole; but the institutions, acting in pursuit of some grudge, refused to have anything to do with him.

Matters were brought to a head when Maxwell made an open offer that either he should be reinstated in charge, or he would make an offer to buy out all shareholders. The offer was at a minimal price, as Maxwell admitted, and shareholders would have been much better advised to accept Captain Bob's return, but the institutions were adamant. Sir Walter attempted to convince Rothschilds and the Bank of England of this, to no avail: he came away grumbling darkly of Ananias and Caiaphas. Norman Freeman, who talked grandly about his responsibility to his funds, marshalled his colleagues into an acceptance of the offer, worth about £2 million.

The sequel is interesting. The journals business, representing the greater part of what was bought back by Maxwell in 1974, was sold by him in 1986 for £238 million. For whatever reasons, but with what seemed to one of us involved at the time nothing better than 'petty vindictiveness', the City establishment united against a man to the clear disadvantage of small shareholders. The Bank of England, which had done much to make the recovery of Pergamon possible, did nothing to ensure a better outcome.

There is one entertaining sidelight to this. One of the objections to the reinstatement of Maxwell was that his activities were the subject of a Board of Trade investigation, the report of which was not issued until October 1973. The investigation had been made by two distinguished gentlemen, Rondle Owen Charles Stable, QC, and Sir Ronald George Leach, CBE,

FCA, who had been appointed in September 1969. Their report, which ran to 664 pages with 437 documents, was highly critical of Maxwell's activities; the inspectors had 'no hesitation in attributing the primary responsibility for the rise and fall of Pergamon to Mr Maxwell'. In view of the hundredfold increase in the value of Pergamon since Robert Maxwell bought it back, not only is this ironic, but the report achieved a unique distinction when it was issued as a command document, by Her Majesty's Stationery Office, with an introductory note by the inspectors:

> We regret that we were in error in stating in paragraph 714 that at the 31 October 1968 R. M. and Co., owed Pergamon £50,809. That sum was in fact owed by Pergamon to R. M. & Co.
>
> All reference in the report to that debt and the state of the account between Pergamon/M. S. I. (1964) and R. M. & Co., at 31 October 1968 are inaccurate and the opinion expressed in paragraph 823 should be disregarded.

Since this confusion in the minds of the inspectors between debtors and creditors invalidated a vital section of the report, any moral force their strictures might have had was very considerably diminished.

No subsequent corporate battle has been so thoroughly followed through, illuminated (after a fashion) by the Department of Trade report and by the continuing skirmishes as City institutions and personalities failed to grasp the basic realities of an industrial enterprise.

It is a measure of the changes in the City that the Pergamon affair would not happen again in the same way. Institutions have become more conscious of their responsibilities towards small shareholders. The Takeover Panel and the Bank are becoming habituated to firm action, even against pillars of the established order. The expensive irrelevance of Department of Trade investigation has been made obvious and, most importantly, the City has as last begun to appreciate the importance of comprehending how industry actually works, and is taking some pains to do so.

PART TWO

City Slickers

5

Takeovers

'The Beaver's best course was, no doubt, to procure
A second-hand dagger-proof coat ...'

LEWIS CARROLL

Pergamon was but the most dramatic of a number of sharply fought inter-company actions that aroused ill will and acrimony among City institutions, and led the Bank of England to intervene in order to define the limits of the acceptable in the takeover business. The recommendations of their working party were embodied in a little yellow book, which became the constant companion of every merchant banker. Recommendations proved hardly enough: some of the chairmen of this world, once having had the error of their ways pointed out, might well be trusted to abide by the code, but the City was becoming inhabited by a more predatory breed, in need of firmer measures, and the Panel on Takeovers and Mergers was established in 1969 to enforce the code. An important principle had been established. City customs were being codified and administered by an independent tribunal, without the force of the law, and relying on the co-operation of those who submitted themselves to it.

It is something of a surprise that the Takeover Panel has worked as well as it has for as long as it has. In part this must be due to Lord Shawcross's ability as chairman in giving it a good start, but also to the willingness in the City to pay heed to the judgements of an authority that could deploy only the most moderate of penalties.

Much of this was a result of the club-like ethos accepted at that time, which relied on an undefined but well-understood set of values. Voluntary societies rarely need more than such an imprecise formulary which, once fixed, may remain unaltered for considerable periods; my own college has had one excellent inhibition since the seventeenth century – undergraduates must not get drunk too often.

If such a system can command allegiance it works smoothly; director-generals come from the ranks of the practitioners themselves and are always available for informal consultation. When an investigation is needed it can be carried out by those who are familiar with the actualities of the market,

33

promptly and cheaply, in all matters quite unlike the practice of the Department of Trade.

The growth of contested takeovers came as welcome news to merchant banks. They were able to add considerably to their fee income, since however large it would necessitate only marginal additional expense. Although in a sporting fashion fees were usually charged on a no-foal-no-fee basis, banks managed to cover their expenses in an abortive bid; and then the successful defending bank would have done extremely well. Since mergers are often accompanied by refinancing, an added benefit comes from the fees charged for the issue of new capital, which may often amount to as much or more than that of the bid itself.

And there was the excitement of it all: corporate finance departments working through the night, correcting drafts coming hourly from the printers, day-long conferences, interviews with the press, all as far removed as possible from the even pattern of banking life where excitement is otherwise invariably the consequence of bad news. Both the profit and the challenge brought talent flocking to merchant banks. Accountants and lawyers could become directors of corporate finance departments in their early thirties. No place existed for any but the best; while a decently competent scion of the family might safely be left, with prudent guidance, to direct other aspects of banking business, the takeover trade demanded personal and intellectual qualities of an unusual level. Many corporate finance men, like Derek Palmar and Christopher Hogg of Hill Samuel, went on to head large companies.

The high level of profits that might be made from a successful coup tempted some of the more aggressive characters into making bids that were quite devoid of industrial logic, for the sole purpose of financial gain, generally by releasing property for development. This process, which became infamous as 'asset-stripping', is associated with the Slater Walker group, although these operations were more generally carried out by such people as Christopher Selmes or John Bentley, protégés of the company founded by Jim Slater and Peter Walker. It is possible to defend asset-stripping as a process which, like shooting admirals, keeps others on their toes, and maximizes return on capital resources; it was the attendant disregard of other interests – workers, customers, and suppliers – that generated most heat. Partly as a result the split became wider between industry in the provinces, who detected in the bright young London men a ruthlessness coupled with a lack of understanding, and the City institutions. Much of the public distrust of the City stems from this period.

After 1974 the takeover business fell off: international lending became the new glamour activity and some of the best-known practitioners, such as Charles Ball of Kleinworts, slipped out of merchant banking.

When it resurfaced ten years later the previous club-like atmosphere had clouded beyond recognition. The original pocket-sized rule book had become a loose-leaf binder, constantly revised, retaining the elements of a consensus but increasingly less authoritative. 'The peer group pressure', as a Bank of England man put it, 'that has kept us more or less in order', had lessened as matters grew in complexity.

Merchant banking infrastructure had altered with the mood. Whereas in the 1960s all accepting houses and issuing houses had felt themselves able to handle mergers and retained at least a rudimentary company finance department, by the 1980s the business was concentrated in four houses. The contrast between merchant banks' specialities became more marked: houses were increasingly known for their corporate finance, international lending or portfolio investment work, rather than for a general high level of banking competence, and as clearing banks moved into these areas the community of interest that had held the accepting houses together declined.

As some banks seemed to have retired from the fray and deployed their energies elsewhere, the competition between those most active in the takeover market grew increasingly animated, and it became clear that takeover battles in the 1980s would be fought with minimal attention to generally accepted rules.

Contested bids have always aroused partisan passions among those engaged on either side, passions not dissimilar to those exhibited in party politics, and which have similar origins.

It is a tribute to man's capacity for sustained self-deception that politicians, however disparate their opinions, remain convinced that the country can flourish only through their remaining in, or securing, office. Only they themselves can get it right, whatever the evidence may seem to the contrary.

Many boards of directors share the same conviction. It is not, one must understand, that they want to retain their own comfortable and lucrative positions, which would be at hazard in a takeover; it is rather that only they really understand the problems of the organization; if their performance has been lacklustre it is about to make a dramatic improvement; if it has been satisfactory, the future lies in peril.

This syndrome is particularly common among the newer, brasher, more opinionated and conceited businessman, as it is among the same sort of politician: examples spring to mind. In the days after the cease-fire had been sounded in the Great Aluminium War takeovers were handled with some circumspection, after long deliberation between boards and their banks and lawyers, who specialized in emitting notes of caution and restraining their more enthusiastic clients. Circumspection is today discredited, and merchant banks such as Morgan Grenfell, once the most restrained of institutions, push matters to the limits even of Bank of England disapproval. Fired by the now enormous sums that can be spent on contested takeovers (the Guinness bid for Distillers was estimated to cost £80 million) advisers spend sleepless nights dreaming of possible victims for their more predatory clients. Once the object is identified the idea is, literally, sold to chairmen who may not at that time stand in any relationship to the adviser proposing it, but who are prepared to pay for the suggestion. Merchant bankers do well; in 1985 Morgan Grenfell's directors nearly doubled their previous year's pay.

Both 1985 and 1986 saw takeover warfare carried out on a scale and with a ferocity hitherto unexampled. The annual value of takeovers and mergers rose from £1.1 billion in 1981 to an average of about £2.3 billion in 1982 and 1983, £5.56 billion in 1984, and is currently (March 1986) running at over £10 billion.

Hanson Trust and United Biscuits were competing in a bid for the Imperial Tobacco Company, which had previously itself intended to merge with United: Guinness and Distillers Co. and Argyll were locked in another tripartite struggle. When the Monopolies and Mergers Commission decided not to go ahead with a reference on the Guinness bid for Distillers, Argyll went to the Court of Appeal in an effort to have the verdict overturned; losing this, they took the matter to the European Court of Human Rights. Furious at what he considered to be an unfair attack from Imperial, Lord Hanson informed his shareholders that

> you have been grossly misled by the inaccuracies in Imperial's advertising campaign against Hanson Trust. We have been left with no alternative but to issue writs against Imperial, each one of its directors and its advertising agents seeking damages for malicious falsehood and defamation ... You must surely ask yourselves what the Imperial board can hope to gain ...

The wrangle over the future of the Westland Helicopter caused an international stir and brought down two Cabinet ministers.

One result of the increased fury of takeovers, not unconnected with the particular desire of chairmen for self-publicity, is the deluge of offensive and defensive advertising that now often appears. Ten years ago these battles were waged by carefully drafted circulars sent to shareholders, supplemented by behind-the-scenes talks with large institutional holders, incessant telephone conversations with financial journalists, and some modest advertising in the City pages.

The cost of takeovers is now swollen by very considerable sums: estimates by advertising agents report that £4 million was spent in the Allied Lyons/Elders bid, nearly £2 million on Burtons/Debenham, and that Guinness was spending £1 million a week to assist in keeping Argyll at bay, some of which went to such unlikely journals as the *Sun* and the *Star*.

This is, of course, the shareholders' money, and it may be wondered if better ways of spending it might not be imagined. It is doubtful whether shareholders are swayed by such methods. They are as capable of working out what is best for them in a bid as they were when they bought the shares in the first place, and their attention is much more likely to be commanded by letters from the board than by the hyperbole of advertising agents. In particular, Distillers shareholders might wonder at the wisdom of offering to pay for the whole of Guinness's costs in mounting their bid, and to what extent this was inspired solely by a concern for their welfare.

Certainly the institutions, who will almost always decide the day in the end, do not appreciate these effusions. Two institutional executives were quoted in the *Financial Times* on 20 February 1986 as saying: 'Shareholders aren't idiots. Advertisements like these simply insult their intelligence. The advertisement industry is supposed to have a code about being legal, decent and honest. These advertisements may be legal, but they are neither decent nor honest.' And 'I find it disturbing, deeply disturbing. Far from swinging shareholders in the board's favour, spending millions of pounds on newspaper advertising, often in newspapers they didn't even read, is much more likely to alienate them.'

Some rather dubious PR methods were employed, although there was suspicion that these were devised by mutual agreement between officially opposed public relations advisers: it was discovered that James Gulliver, chairman of Argyll, had claimed in his *Who's Who* biography to have been educated at Harvard on the strength of a three-weeks course he had attended there; since no man is on his oath in *Who's Who*, and since Mr Gulliver had a perfectly good degree from Georgia Tech, an institution of considerable eminence, this was felt to be unsporting. Honours ended even, after a great many more column inches.

Tempers truly flared in an episode of clashes between GEC and Plessey in their takeover battle when GEC accused Plessey of issuing 'a document which would have done credit to Dr Goebbels' and was 'a caricature of GEC'. GEC expressed themselves disillusioned with the panel's ability to act decisively to restrain such comment, although on many previous occasions warnings had been issued by the panel on the subject of inaccurate and misleading information circulating in bids, and 'draconian action' threatened.

Exactly what draconian action the Panel had within its powers to deploy is unclear; as with puddle-making puppies it is not much use punishing long after the event. In takeovers immediate action, hour by hour, is essential. The Panel admitted its own limitations, one official being quoted by the *Financial Times* in February 1986 as saying that 'when people reach for their lawyers, and start suing each other then the Panel steps back'. A banker commented at the same time that

> 2 or 3 years ago practitioners observed the spirit of the takeover code and the Stock Exchange rules and feared the two bodies. Nowadays, the form is not to consult them, if you're thinking of doing something marginal, but to just go ahead, knowing the authorities will be too feeble to do anything about it.

At that time the panel had just acquired a new director-general, John Walker-Haworth, a civilized and properly cynical man who justified himself by bringing out with commendable speed regulations to restrain future advertising, and pronounced firmly: 'People have forgotten what our requirements are and we have said enough is enough.' Like any of the panel's regulations, advertising restraints lack the force of law, but have other advantages: they possessed the considerable counteradvantage of having been produced in a speedy fashion, within days of the problem appearing. Any rules having legal effect, capable of being challenged in the courts, would inevitably have taken much longer. Yet it would take a temerarious adviser to defy these rules, knowing that to do so would forfeit future goodwill and invite that very legal restraint that the bolder spirits are especially concerned to avoid. There is little to be gained by winning a skirmish if one's forces are thereby weakened for any future campaign.

The new rules had the added merit of being clearly intelligible: all advertisements during the course of a bid were banned unless they fell into exempt non-controversial categories or had previously been submitted to the panel for approval. The Bank of England intervened quickly in a more direct way when Morgan Grenfell bought on behalf of its clients shares in bid-for companies, at a total cost far exceeding Morgan's own capital value; the Bank considered that this was an inappropriate and excessive exposure.

Both these actions, while being timely beyond anything that might be expected from government action, did not altogether succeed in suppressing public disquiet. Shareholders were divided: if a bid is successful the shareholders of the company being taken over are happy enough, seeing good profit on their investment. Those of the losing bidder may also have the consolation of seeing their company making a windfall profit by selling their, usually large, share in the victim's equity. But the owners of the successful bidder have witnessed their board being blackguarded, often convincingly, and a very great deal of their money siphoned off to pay advisers, while having to rely on the future to produce less-than-certain profits. Small wonder that in such cases many vote with their feet and sell up.

Politicians had the bad old Slater Walker days vividly brought to mind, and hankered after firmer controls. Even the minister responsible for preparing the Financial Services Bill, Alex Fletcher, was reported as considering that

the Panel will need to be a stronger and more professional body than ever before if it is to cope with the pressures that today's megabids have brought to the City.

There can be no doubt that the arrival in Britain of poison-pill tactics, commercial espionage or dirty tricks, excessive, indeed profligate, advertising add up to the most ungentlemanly conduct and do nothing to enhance the City's reputation. All the regulations should make it abundantly clear that they are determined to clamp down on these foreign imports.

On the other hand Mr Fletcher approved recourse to the courts, an inevitable result of which is to remove matter from the jurisdiction of the Panel.

A real dilemma exists: if recourse to the law is to be allowed, the powers of a regulatory body must be limited to whatever internal sanctions it may muster; if it is to have real powers of control it must have these in a statutory form, and be a prosecuting agency. It must, in effect, be the equivalent of the SEC (the Securities Exchange Commission of the United States).

This destroys the whole concept of self-regulation by practitioners. The questions that had been current during the asset-stripping activities of the 70s were raised again. Even if it be admitted – and the lack of proof has been mentioned – that takeovers do in fact improve the productivity of industry, there are some important glosses to be made.

Most industries have something that looks very like a natural rate of growth. This can vary greatly between industries – new products and technologies obviously advancing much more rapidly than those with established markets and products, but in any one company much of the board's energies are devoted to keeping growth in balance. Investment cannot be allowed to outrun earnings (but it is suicidal to neglect investment for short-term earnings); market penetration must go hand in hand with product and service availability (but new markets must be tested); skilled workers and management must constantly be recruited (but idle talent cannot be left around to become frustrated). And the constant pressure of the market to produce earnings and dividend growth must be reckoned with.

Many boards breathed sighs of relief when dividends were statutorily curbed; earnings could be retained and reinvested without having to be distributed to clamorous shareholders, regarded as a necessity but a regrettable one. (Few members of the Socialist Workers' Party can feel a stronger antipathy to the distribution of dividends than do professional managers, conscious of so many necessary investments they see clamouring for attention.) The industrious took this dividend restraint as an opportunity for re-equipment: the idle as a blessed interlude of peace.

Contested takeover bids were a violent interruption to this seemly order of things. I fought a number of these, attacking and defending, and contrived with greater decency some agreed mergers. All were understood to be based on industrial logic; one might argue (and did fiercely) about figures, but the logic of the case was vital. Future strategy had to be clear, down to the deployment of machine tools and sales agencies. The backing of one's own workforce had to be secured (though rather out of common sense and self-preservation than as a matter of doctrine). Any tendency to cut corners would be frowned on by advisers, anxious to avoid being tarred with the asset-stripping brush. Virtue was often its own reward, since mergers that exhibited a clear strategy also tended to be successful.

It used to be necessary, in a rather-too-gentlemanly City and in an industrial climate where management often lacked a clear sense of purpose, to remind boards that their first duty was to their shareholders, and that this involved maximizing the profitability of the enterprise. Today it is more often necessary to remind management that profitability is only one of the objectives they are set and that they must operate under constraints. Boundaries of the acceptable have been fixed for some time; the selling of adulterated goods has been frowned upon (but some manufacturers still sail near the wind by selling doubtful products justified under the guise of a need for 'eye appeal' or 'shelf life'); the use of slave labour is no longer tolerated. Today Barclays find that profits from South Africa are similarly deemed 'inadmissible'. Rupert Murdoch's policy of staff relations causes eyebrows to be raised. Even the Bank of England points out some of the possibly deleterious effects that the takeover boom may have. It might also be mentioned that the predators are not always those who make the most useful contributions to their industry and society. James Gulliver's abilities have benefited his shareholders, but the leaders in quality and service remain the staider and more conventional firms of Sainsbury, Waitrose and Marks & Spencer. It is not a coincidence either that such companies are known for sound management practices and decent staff relations.

Although the emergence of contested takeover bids has had profound, if unclear, consequences for British industry and for the City, even the largest bid is a domestic squabble. Unless they be particularly cantankerous, or the companies involved have foreign connections British takeover battles raise no interest abroad, do nothing for external earning nor add to the capacity of City institutions in the world market.

The present international importance of the City stems directly from a different source, and one also significantly influenced by Siegmund Warburg.

6

A New Currency

It could not be accounted surprising that the post-war Labour government remained enamoured of the apparatus of regulation and control it inherited from the wartime coalition, and indeed that it should add to these rules in profusion. It was however odd that the Conservative governments that came to power after 1951 took so little action to mend matters. Even some food rationing remained in place for a year or two, building material restrictions for several, while exchange controls, especially in the electorally annoying limitations on individual expenditure abroad, stayed in force until abolished by the first Thatcher government, thirty-four years after the end of the war. Nor did any government think twice about imposing arbitrary, confusing and often downright conflicting series of direct controls on domestic credit spending, by banks, hire-purchase companies, and finance houses. In spite of this battery of government controls in the aftermath of a devastating war the City of London was able to become, once again, and remain, the undisputed centre of international finance.

The reasons were complex. One, and a not unimportant one, is natural and geographic. International time zones enable London to overlap the end of the day's trading on the Far Eastern exchanges and the beginning of the day in New York, enabling a 24-hour international market to be operated from London. The same characteristic is of course shared with Paris, but here London's second advantage is clear. The last successful invasion of England was in 1066, and since then a rule of law has evolved that has enabled trading to continue undisturbed. Even Magna Carta can be invoked in aid of commercial equity (as is currently being done by those who want wine bars to observe the charter's provision that 'there shall be one measure of ale and wine in the realm'): the Bank of England and Lloyd's are approaching their tercentenary; the Stock Exchange has been functioning for nearly as long. France, in a mere two centuries, has had three royal, two imperial and five republican constitutions, three revolutions and four foreign invasions. A tranquil life is much valued by financiers.

In Switzerland, a possible contender, and one sharing stable political conditions, banking is divided between the cantonal centres of Zurich, Geneva, Basle and Berne, with two languages between them, and a jealously guarded system which regulates narrowly the establishment of foreign banks and employment of foreign nationals.

By contrast, ever since Oliver Cromwell welcomed the return of the Jews, British governments have encouraged open access to the markets (only two of the accepting houses were *not* founded by Jewish, German, French or American families) and have avoided differentiating between banks on grounds of ownership.

Perhaps most important of all is the attractiveness of London as a place to work in. This may sound odd to provincial Englishmen who regard the capital as a sink of iniquity of rapidly increasing unpleasantness but, compared with New York, it is infinitely more comfortable for the man of moderate means. One of the difficulties that have faced American banks for years is the near-impossibility of prising staff out of the London office for postings back home. Only Paris can compare in agreeableness, but Americans in particular find the habits and traditions of the business community unsympathetic; chauvinism is, after all, a French invention.

None of these factors would have proved decisive had not a form of finance, that has since proved enormously popular, evolved in London rather than elsewhere: as it was, Paris very nearly reaped the benefits.

Siegmund Warburg may not perhaps be given all the credit for developing the Eurodollar market: oddly enough the historical primacy can probably be given to the Russians who, rather than hold dollars in the US, deposited them with Banque Commerciale pour l'Europe du Nord in Paris – telex address Eurobank – and other city figures such as Sir George Bolton of BOLSA took up the idea with great enthusiasm.

The genesis of Eurodollars (the term quite simply means US dollars held outside the US) – lies in the post-war economy. Although the USA was experiencing boom conditions the government, in financing military expenditure abroad, first in Korea and later in Vietnam, was also running an external deficit. Most of the dollars spent abroad stayed there; the dollar looked reliable, and until 1958 sterling remained unconvertible. Long-term international finance before the war had been denominated almost exclusively in sterling. After 1945 the dollar was the obvious alternative, and by the mid 1950s the owners of dollars held abroad were looking hard for interesting outlets. It was Siegmund Warburg who found the first major one.

In 1956 René Mayer, president of the European Coal and Steel Commission, asked Warburg to place a $40 million loan on behalf of the commission. Once an American insurance company had been persuaded to lead with 5 per cent of the total the remainder came easily enough, and was the first long-term loan, denominated in dollars, to be raised for a European institution and subscribed largely from European sources. Within two years Warburg had also arranged dollar loans for the Republic of Austria, Jamaica, and his old friends British Aluminium.

Although the money came mainly from abroad, these loans were made through Warburg's American connections, and it was 1963 before the first medium-term dollar loan was raised outside the US for a foreign borrower. The agreement was for Autostrade Italiane, the subsidiary of the Italian state holding company IRI, one of Mussolini's more successful creations, to borrow $15 million for six years: the contract was signed in Holland, under English law, for an Italian company, the loan issued in Luxembourg in American dollars.

Luxembourg was chosen because the Governor of the Bank of England, Lord Cromer, was personally doubtful about the merits of the idea. The Bank accordingly proposed to levy a stamp duty on the transaction which Siegmund avoided by making the issue in Luxembourg. Lord Cromer was fortunately later persuaded, largely by Sir George Bolton, to relax his initial negative stand and agreed that future loans of this sort would not be penalized. Nor was the market at first any less suspicious: the issue proved difficult to place, and had to be discounted to attract subscribers.

The first Eurodollar loans were all arranged for non-Americans; it was not until 1965 that the first American institution, Cyanamid, made use of the new market. After that events conspired to assure the growth of the Eurodollar market. Foreign expenditure during the Vietnam war, with the consequent outflow of dollars, led to restrictions on the part of the US government such as Regulation Q. This set interest ceilings on deposits, and sent depositors off to London in search of higher returns. Borrowers had to follow.

The American government began to commit the same errors that British governments had previously made but were now busily repairing – attempting to circumscribe financial activities by legislation. It was the Kennedy administration that went near to depriving New York of its natural place as the centre of world capitalism by imposing on 18 July 1963 the Interest Equalization Tax, intended to put a stop to the flow of dollars leaving the US, but having the effect of making sure that no dollar ever got repatriated there. US corporations were driven to issuing foreign securities by the limitation imposed under the 1964 voluntary credit restraint programme. Interest equalization tax, effective the same year, penalized American investors who bought foreign securities and so effectively banned the American market to foreign investors. The cumulative effect of these measures was to stop the development of US banking dead in its tracks, and ensure that international finance went elsewhere.

It was possible that the new market might well have emerged in Paris rather than London. Morgans, who had already arranged a DM loan in Paris, were negotiating with a Japanese company to raise a $15 million loan in France. Fortunately for London the Bank of France proved even less amenable than the Bank of England, and placed so many difficulties in the way that the loan was not concluded until November 1963, by which time Warburg had put themselves firmly in the lead.

The market developed gradually; another thirteen loans in 1963, totalling less than $150 million, including Warburg issues for the City of Oslo and the ECSC, rising to $680 million in 1964, and to only $800 million in 1965. Each loan still necessitated long negotiations with regulatory authorities and lenders still uncertain about exactly what it was they were engaging in.

Growth remained steady rather than spectacular until the oil price rise after 1973 provoked an influx of oil money, which still refused to find its way to the US. In 1974 $14 billion ended up in American banks, while $23 billion went to the Eurodollar market, $7 billion to European banks and $11 billion to Third-World countries. From that time onward a substantial slice of American capital markets have remained abroad, with London the centre of management. It is not perhaps going too far to suggest that it is this factor alone which has buttressed the City's position as a centre of international banking.

7

The Plastic Bankers

'There, London's voice: "Get money still!
And then let virtue follow if she will." '

ALEXANDER POPE

In 1971 Wm Brandt's Sons & Co. Ltd, one of the founding members of the Accepting Houses Committee, founded in Archangel in the eighteenth century and established in London since 1805, since when it had remained almost entirely a family affair, came under the direct control of National & Grindlays Bank. The existing management was replaced, the partners' room stripped, the mahogany staircase destroyed, and shiny plastic surfaces were employed to convey an impression of vibrant modern banking. The change could be taken to symbolize the rapid elevation to a new style of aggressive and animated financial entrepreneurs, hardly, however, more successful than their predecessors, for their decline was to be even more rapid. In common with less ancient houses, Brandt's, under its new management, overextended its resources and came to the point of collapse within three years: a collapse which those who had been displaced saw as almost inevitable.

At about the same time plastics made their appearance in banking in a somewhat different context. Written instruments of exchange have been the currency of commerce since Ancient Egypt; it was only in 1965 that their eventual supersession was initiated. In that year the Westminster Bank bought a significant majority shareholding in Diners' Club, to be followed the next year by Barclays' introduction of the Barclaycard, making the advent of a new method of credit transfer. Cheque cards, which enabled the use of cheques to become more widespread, rapidly became popular: the first cash dispenser – which was the first in the world – made its appearance in 1967 nurtured by similar cards. Plastic money had come to stay.

These two events may be taken as symbolic of more fundamental changes which are still affecting the City, although their significance was overlooked at the time. The most obvious movement in the financial world was that of the clearing banks towards conjunction, a traditional remedy at times of stress. The National Provincial bought out District Bank in 1962 and merged with the Westminster six years later. Barclays acquired the fine old Liverpool bank of Martins the same year. In 1970 Williams & Glyn's was created by a merger of Williams Deacon's, Glyn Mills and National Bank, and the National Commercial Banking Group. In a move of doubtful wisdom Barclays and Lloyds tried to merge, but were prevented by the Monopolies Commission. The Midland Bank attempted to break away from the cartel, but was restrained by that pillar of free enterprise, Reginald Maudling.

None of this looked likely to be very effective against the background of marked decline in the clearers' share of banking business. Even the banks themselves were beginning to notice that they were losing deposits to the building societies at a rapidly increasing rate. In the ten years between 1948 and 1958 building societies' share of all deposits doubled from 7 to 15 per cent and to 25 per cent in the following decade, while the clearing banks' share dropped from 44 to 40 and 31 per cent respectively; the banks retained their share of the less profitable interest-bearing deposits, the building societies expanding at the expense of national savings (see Table 3).

Table 3 Shares of Interest-bearing UK deposits prior to 1971 (percentage)

Year	London clearing banks	Other banks	Building societies	National Savings	Trustee Savings banks
1921	46	–	6	47	1
1930	39	–	16	42	2
1938	33	–	24	39	3
1948	24	–	12	62	1
1958	27	–	24	45	3
1968	26	2	36	30	6
1979	21	6	46	22	5

Institute of Bankers

These were matters of some seriousness. Clearing banks looked upon themselves not only – or sometimes even primarily – as commercial organizations but rather as public services for the transmission of money; and this indeed was so. British retail banking developed a money transfer service which is still unmatched, as anyone who has ever tried to cash a cheque drawn on an out-of-state bank in the USA has experienced. Something like 60 per cent of clearing bank staff are engaged in providing these services; rather more than 60,000 million such transactions take place every year. The banks act as agents for the Bank of England in distributing and collecting cash; 15,000 branches throughout the country operate a collection and distribution system. This expensive network was at least in part paid for by balances left in customers' current accounts, on which no interest was paid, and on deposit accounts, which carried only low rates. To lose such deposits at the rate that was becoming apparent in the 1960s presented a cause for concern.

The clearing banks showed little sign of appreciating their danger, and in what looked like terminal self-destructive throes, succumbing to staff pressure, made things even easier for the competition in 1969 by closing all their branches on Saturdays. It seemed as though complacent stagnation could go no further, but in fact 1969 marked a turning-point in the clearers' self-awareness, from which much else sprang.

As the building societies nibbled away at the banks' small deposits a different threat was emerging at the opposite end of the scale. This was that inter- and extra-bank lending that has become known as the 'wholesale' money market. Originally stimulated by the requirement that local authorities borrow part of their finance in the open market rather than obtaining it all from central government, the wholesale market developed independently from clearing banks. Rates were higher than for bank deposits, but transactions in the wholesale markets were unsecured.

The wholesale market produced two new types of institutions: finance brokers, who acted as intermediaries, and quasi-banks, who took in money market deposits to lend on at higher rates, generally to property companies. Both these attracted lively and aggressive personalities from unconventional – in City terms – backgrounds, who were regarded with a mixture of distaste and amusement by those already established. As well as being profitable it was also the easiest thing in the world for anyone who wished to chance their arm in the financial world to set up what they might have called a bank, requiring little more than an office, a telephone, and a confident manner in order to take one's place alongside the Rothschilds and the Lazards.

Such secondary banks and other financial institutions were not licensed by the Bank of England, but by the Board of Trade under section 123 of the Companies Act, 1967, and were hence known as 123-banks. The purpose of the Act was originally to clarify the position of such institutions as finance houses that were neither banks nor moneylenders, and to give a licence to those who were 'bona fide carrying out the business of banking'. The Board of Trade was not required to carry out continuing supervision, but merely to allow companies to escape the restrictive provisions of the moneylending laws. The opportunity was however too good to miss; companies rapidly applied for the new status and by 1970 eighty-seven certificates had been issued, rising to 133 by 1973.

The department known in recent times as the Board of Trade, Department of Trade, or the Department of Trade and Industry, is one of the largest, but hardly one of the most highly regarded, departments of state. Enthusiastic recruits to the administrative grades of the Civil Service do not eagerly clamour to be posted to assist in its departmental functions, which include an omnium gatherum of responsibilities for industries not the responsibility of other ministries, consumer affairs and the legal framework for the regulation of industrial and commercial enterprises, including insolvency.

Although the President of the Board of Trade traditionally ranks high in Cabinet, directly after the Foreign Secretary and the Chancellor of the Exchequer, the post is rarely given to a politician thought of as powerful, and has in recent years, even when united with the Department of Industry, seen its ministers being treated as pawns in Cabinet affairs, and changed with embarrassing rapidity; by 1986 there have been five in as many years. When on its own the Department of Trades' Civil Servants have ranked lower in service terms than their contemporaries – in 1982 for example both the Permanent Under-Secretary and Deputy Under-Secretary, were Companions of the Order of the Bath, rather than Knights, which they might have expected to be in another department.

It was in that capacity of general government dogsbody that the Department of Trade was landed with the responsibility for deciding on the suitability of organizations to receive licences to operate as banks, a task for which it was unsuited and ill-equipped.

The Bank of England had to be consulted, but was not in a position to be very helpful, partly due to its not being staffed to the necessary level, having but fifteen people in a department overseeing more than three hundred banks, but also since many of the new 123-banks were not the sort of people whom Bank of England officials were used to coping with. Having dealt with recognizable bankers with predictable habits of thought they were not able to understand the likes of Mr William Stern and Mr John Bentley, or Mr Tom Whyte.

The Board of Trade officials were even more removed from the sticky business; all the under-secretaries at the head of the relevant divisions had gone straight from Oxford to Cambridge into the Civil Service, escaping all taint of any commercial experience. They were not in a position to make fine judgements, and appeared not even to try. Margaret Reid in her book on the *Secondary Banking Crisis* quotes a senior police officer as saying: 'They just dished the certificates out to all and sundry.'

This may be unjust: the Civil Service does nothing without adequate documentation, and applicants were made to fill out a lengthy questionnaire. It may well be that the department placed greater reliance on the Bank of England's scrutiny than it would rightly bear, but it is certain that, as Michael Moran says, 'the Board of Trade looked only for "a minimum level of banking characteristics" and felt no obligation to supervise the activities of certified institutions. In this way many banks disappeared from the sight of supervision into the crevices between administrative agencies.' Many of the 123-banks were in fact perfectly respectable, being subsidiaries of foreign banks or clearing banks or, like Cripps Warburg and Edward Bates, were run by experienced people of the highest reputation. Some, such as one dubious institution sponsored by an absconding Member of Parliament, were not.

Conditions in the late 1960s and early 1970s proved ideal for the forced growth of these exotic plants. The Barber boom (a description that irritates Lord Barber, who has since maintained he thought the level of public spending that fuelled the dash for growth, and the raging inflation that followed, too high, and that it was his colleagues that insisted on the policy: but he continued as Chancellor) made investment in property irresistible. As prices rose with hitherto undreamt of rapidity it seemed a matter of little import that developers should pay unprecedentedly high rates and that the lending banks should make correspondingly high profits. The whole episode exemplified the nursery adage 'don't encourage them, or they'll get too excited, and it will all end in tears'. They did, and it did. Some established banks cheered on the 123-banks and others emulated them. The spanking new house of Slater Walker blinded many experienced eyes, being courted as a partner by such large and well-established institutions as Hill Samuel; a few weeks before its collapse a senior Bank of England official was still to be heard saying that 'there never has been, and is not now, any necessity for "lifeboat" support of Slater Walker'.

Established reputations were disregarded in favour of the new. The former Chancellor of the Exchequer, Reginald Maudling, felt able to launch the Real Estate Fund of America in London as 'a good and sound investment' even although its principal, Jerome Hoffman, had already been banned from the securities business by the US attorney general for 'reckless, improvident and fraudulent' behaviour.

Gramco, a no less adventurous enterprise, was backed by E. D. Sassoon and Credit Commercial, assisted by the Westminster Bank, and many distinguished merchant banks. Bernie Cornfeld, the founder of Investors' Overseas Services, convinced many who ought to have known better that it was enough 'sincerely to want to be rich'.

Political change accompanied and reinforced the new mood of adventurous acquisitiveness. By 1971 the City was feeling its oats, having been bruised by the systems of credit control that Labour governments had found it necessary to implement and irritated with the Bank of England for its role in enforcing them. A change of government was eagerly welcomed; established banks had seen substantial parts of their business filched by the new institutions who, either officially or unofficially, were less rigidly controlled; much effort was spent in discovering ways of circumventing restrictions; the clearing banks were still smarting at the epithet of 'soporific' bestowed on them by the Monopolies and Mergers Commission and deeply resented jokes about lettuce at luncheon inflicted on them by their richer customers.

They were then very ready to accept the decision made by the Conservative government in 1971 to abolish the system of both 'quantitative' controls, which regulated how much they might lend, and 'qualitative' controls, which dictated to whom advances might be made. At the same time those cartel agreements which had been in existence between the clearing banks for generations, and that between the discount houses themselves and with the clearing banks on Treasury Bill bids were abolished. The clearing banks renounced their privilege under Section VII of the 1947 Companies Act and agreed to disclose their true profits.

From henceforth competition was to be the watchword; profitability a prime target, and security a secondary issue; marketing was the topic on all lips.

Left to themselves the clearers could do little quickly: they were staffed by the same cautious and disciplined managers with habits formed by a lifetime of prudent lending. Lacking professional personnel management and experienced negotiators, and harassed by the growing power of staff unions, the convenience of customers was allowed to become neglected. Overnight change was impossible to organizations of the clearers' size and entrenched prejudices, but they could at least share in the exciting game by lending, directly or through the money market, very large sums indeed to the new men.

With the new men came new manners: I once met a white-faced and speechless senior manager who had just returned from submitting a perfectly respectable loan proposal to his chief executive. The proposal carried a one and a quarter per cent margin; he had been met with what seemed to him a brutal rejection: 'F . . . one and a quarter, I can get 4 on property loans.'

Others possessed more by way of charm, as well as a great deal of ability. Pat Matthews of First National Finance built up an organization that teetered on the brink of collapse but later and in other hands flourished; Jack Delal and Edward du Cann at Keyser Ullman had shown considerable innovative ability. The bigger banks were happy to lend to such companies, and institutions to invest in them: and other less distinguished

51

enterprises could borrow in the market at higher rates but with not much less facility.

The euphoria was shortlived, and nemesis dramatic, but brought with it a profitable lesson. Those who, distrusting the capacity of City organizations to manage the corporate affairs of the City, press for direct government control, would do well to reflect on the lessons of the secondary banking crisis of 1973–4. When the 123-section banks that had been called into existence by the 1967 Companies Act found themselves in difficulties, it was not the Board of Trade, whose licences they held, who took a lead, but the Bank of England.

The Barber boom had been followed by the Heath U-turn, which produced a rise in interest rates from 7 1/2 to 11 1/2 per cent in two weeks and ended with a record MLR (Minimum Lending Rate) of 13 per cent. Its first public victim was Cedar Holdings, established in 1958 as a 'bank', insurance, mortgage and finance agents business. Cedar had appeared to be one of the boom's beneficiaries, with profit and assets of £87,000 and £8 million respectively in 1965, rising to £1.9 million and £128 million in 1973. It was backed by Barclays Bank, had strong institutional shareholders, and was run by gentlemen who, although respectable, would hardly be recognizable as what was then known as 'bankers'. It had been, however, recognized as a bank by the Board of Trade under Section 123. By December 1973 it was in serious trouble; funds had been mismatched, depositors had withdrawn and a stock exchange suspension was imminent unless substantial further sums were found.

Cedar's problems were brought to the Bank of England and a meeting convened for 9 a.m. on 19 December 1973: it continued until 3 a.m. the following day. After a meeting at times acerbic, some of the banks believing they were being asked to pay for the imprudence of others less cautious, the deputy governor, Sir Jasper Hollom, aided by that tower of commonsense and diplomacy in times of stress, Kenneth Cork, had persuaded banks, institutions and shareholders into a settlement involving some £72 million of new money.

The thought of Whitehall having to solve such a problem is inconceivable. No Civil Servant would have the authority or experience, or even share a common language with the bankers or industrialists. A minister would have to be found, briefed, withdrawn from parliamentary duties; and the record of ministers at that department is not such as to fill one with confidence as to the outcome.

The announcement of the Cedar Holdings débâcle lit the fuse for an avalanche of withdrawals; the whole of the secondary banking system was under pressure and, directly or indirectly owing hundreds of millions to the clearing banks, put those institutions themselves into danger. It took

Gordon Richardson, the new Governor, ninety minutes on 21 December to reach agreement with the clearing banks to launch the 'Lifeboat' as the support operation became known. The lifeboat stayed afloat for some years, and rescued many who would otherwise have perished. Eventually £1,300 million was advanced, in addition to an unknown extra sum extended by the banks directly to property customers; estimates of £3,000 million as a whole have been suggested. With a great deal of patience and hard work, with the clearing banks providing management as well as cash, most of this has been recovered, and the best of the secondary banks preserved.

There is not much question but that action of this quality was needed. George Blunden, who later assumed responsibility for supervision of the Bank of England and a man not given to hyperbole, later remarked:

> Without these supporting operations virtually all of the 30 secondary banks in the lifeboat would have collapsed and the cumulative effect of those collapsed would have spread much more widely through the banking system. Undoubtedly many of the primary banks would have been swept away in the maelstrom. As it was, by protecting the secondary banks the Bank of England and the clearing banks ensured that not one of the inner ring of primary banks had to be supported.

The possibility of a widespread collapse was clearly indicated when National Westminster, the second biggest clearing bank, was the victim of unsubstantiated rumours that nevertheless necessitated the issue of a denial by the chairman, and when the Crown Agents, who had been involved in some decidedly dubious business, did in fact near the point of insolvency.

Although it is literally impossible for a department of state to emulate the speed and decisiveness of such an operation it may be argued that government is sovereign and may force its demands through. Quite apart from the obvious rejoinder that this takes time, which is in such crises the rarest of commodities, such demands can only be enforced over the objections of shareholders by the ultimate step of nationalization, the arguments against which scarcely need to be rehearsed.

The Bank might be justly criticized for some weakness in supervision during the secondary banking affair – some of the banks involved were, as the Governor put it, 'proper banks', (a revealing phrase) benefiting from discount-office monitoring, such as Slater Walker, to which the Bank continued to give support when the writing was clear on the wall, and Edward Bates, and in its lack of scrutiny of the 123-licences passed on for comment by the Board of Trade. But in reaching timely decisions at the moment of crisis, and pushing these through, the Bank of England, once armed with unparalleled statutory powers, but thrice blessed with experience and knowledge, proved a uniquely effective instrument for ensuring stability.

The secondary banking crisis left the City confirmed in the conviction that its future could only be secured under the aegis of the Bank, and that government departments had shown themselves wholly unreliable, a conviction which lies at the root of the present division on monitoring the City's affairs.

8

Johnson Matthey

'...London, that great sea, whose ebb and flow
At once is deaf and loud, and on the shore
Vomits its wrecks, and still howls on for more.'

SHELLEY

With the secondary banking crisis safely disposed of, and many of the more picturesque characters of the drama having found alternative employment, the Bank of England lost no time in making sure that as far as possible no such thing would occur again. James Keogh, the existing principal of the Discount Office, the department which had traditionally been responsible for banking supervision, a genial Irishman well known in the City, took a secondary part in the lifeboat, which was directed within the Bank by George Blunden, an executive director. A new department, the Banking and Money Market Supervision (BAMMS) was established, with a staff of seventy, now increased to a hundred; the Discount Office had made do with fifteen, a measure of how far standards of control have been tightened.

Opinion was generally firm that the Department of Trade should be excluded from any future responsibility, and that there should be a clear distinction between 'proper' banks and less worthy establishments. Banks proper could continue to be monitored in the old informal way, while the 'second division' should be subject to more stringent checks by the expanded BAMMS department.

Other central banks paid the Bank of England the compliment of imitation; stimulated by the Bankhaus Herstatt collapse of 1974, which after a worrying and messy interval left many creditors with heavy losses, the governors of the other central banks agreed to establish an international supervisory committee, generally known as the Cooke Committee, after its chairman, Peter Cooke of the Bank of England, with the task of defining a system of agreed international standards.

It took, as might be expected, some time for the British government to formalize matters, and it was not until 1979 that a new Act was passed, doing away with the Section VII and 123-classifications and drawing a

55

line between authorized banks and other institutions, to be known as licensed deposit takers (LDT,) which were not allowed to describe themselves as banks.

The lines of distinction were fluid, enabling an institution with a capital as small as £250,000 to be registered as a bank if it carried out a specialized business. There was some anxiety among the smaller banks (which I participated in as a director of Henry Ansbacher, an authorized bank which was nevertheless felt to be too near the dividing line for comfort) since the status of LDT was seen to be markedly inferior. Although it was understood that a progression to full banking recognition was a possible step if all things went well (George Blunden referred to a 'cursus honorum'), Ansbacher's management would have been deeply chagrined to find themselves initially ranked as an LDT, and were correspondingly relieved when the authorized status was confirmed.

The new BAMMS division kept a watchful eye on the LDTs, but contented themselves with setting capital ratios and requiring quarterly reports from the other more respectable institutions. Even the capital ratios were regarded as desirable, rather than mandatory; banks were expected to show willingness to progress towards them, but were not too strongly criticized if they failed to achieve the minimum standards.

The Bank of England felt that 'proper' banks could be relied upon; trouble had come from the fringe in the past, and was expected to be found there in the future.

As things turned out the Old Lady was proved wrong. It was the respectable, authorized banks who were to cause the severest difficulties, and in doing so illustrate the deficiencies of the 1979 Act, and indicate some previously undetected weaknesses in the financial system.

These lessons were learned quickly; the Act looks likely to become one of the shortest-lived pieces of legislation to reach the Statute Book, since its successor is already in White Paper form, a fact which underlines both the unsatisfactory nature of the Act itself and the considerable changes in the industry which have since ensued.

Some of the biggest banks had well-publicized difficulties in the early 1980s: Midland was put into a dangerous position by the losses piled up in its American acquisition, the Crocker National Bank (see Part Three), and a takeover by the Australia and New Zealand Bank was needed to rescue Grindlays from an unpleasant situation.

It was, however, as often happens, from an unexpected source that the worst trouble emerged, when the Johnson Matthey scandal broke in October 1984.

The Johnson Matthey affair proved unlike previous bank crises in some significant aspects, the most important of which stemmed from the nature of the organization itself. The institutions in trouble in the 1970s were banks or quasi-banks, sometimes odd enough but recognizably discrete financial entities; Johnson Matthey (Bankers) was anything but. Its parent company Johnson Matthey plc was and remains an important international company, well up among the hundred largest of the UK, with assets, in 1984, of some £450 million and a turnover of £1,357 million. With subsidiaries in seventeen different countries, employing 5,779 in the UK alone, it had by 1980 some ninety years of trading behind it. The group was prominent in refining and marketing platinum and platinum products for industry, developing and producing industrial catalysts, and manufacturing gas generating equipment. Pigments, colours and transfers, especially for ceramics, and air pollution control systems, were important products; jewellery was manufactured on a commercial scale; the company traded in base metals on the London Metal Exchange, and the traditional business of producing and dealing in bullion flourished; somewhere, concealed in the ramifications of this organization, was a very small bank.

The operations of JM plc were divided into seven groups; Metals, Printing, Colours, Refining and chemicals, Banking, North America, and Finance and administration. 'Banking' was something of a misnomer, since by far the greatest part of this business was bullion dealing, with banking only occupying the most modest of roles. Bullion was what counted, and it was for its membership of the London gold price fixing that JM was internationally known. Five participants, Johnson Matthey, Samuel Montagu, Mocatta and Goldsmid, Sharps Pixley and Rothschilds, formed a City aristocracy of an arcane and glamorous nature. Meeting twice a day in Rothschilds, they decided the price of gold throughout the world. A ritual took place, with each dealer sitting in his accustomed place, a Union flag before him which he might raise if he wished to halt the proceedings while consulting by telephone with his office. Once agreement was reached by the five the international price of gold was fixed until the next meeting.

Like so many other City institutions the bullion market has undergone a profound change. Until 1968 the Bank of England had, with the agreement of the other central banks, operated the international gold pool through its mechanism; after all South Africa, the source – except for the Soviet Union – of the world gold supplies, was content to sell through this market. In that year, however, the Washington agreement established a free pricing system, and the price of gold, which for years had been fixed at about $35 an ounce, was able to move with trading conditions. It has since been as high as $700 and now moves around $340 an ounce. The central importance of London fixing declined, but Johnson Matthey, by virtue of its industrial custom, remained a force in the bullion market.

There were one or two misadventures, such as a £7 million loss in 1970, but the company continued as a respected leader in this activity, under the solid figure of Lord Robens as chairman.

And it flourished: in the five years between 1976 and 1980 the group's profits rose from £15 to £38.6 million, and in the latter year Lord Robens was able to report:

> For the second year in succession Johnson Matthey Bankers Ltd and its subsidiaries produced a record. A high proportion of the profit was earned from bullion and metal dealing during the second half of the year which was probably the most active trading period in the history of metal markets ... the earnings from bullion dealing overshadow but do not detract from the excellent performance of the bank in its other activities.
>
> Apart from the earnings success, there were two other notable achievements. Although our bank has been an authorised bank and authorised depository since April 1967, it was required, along with all other banks established and operating in this country, to make formal application to the Bank of England to be recognized as a bank under the Banking Act 1979. This recognition was granted ...

At that time the Bank of England, as required by the Act, would have examined the nature of the banking business, and satisfied itself as to the services offered and the competence and probity of the bank's directors and officers. This should have been a searching examination by a regulatory authority determined that, unlike the Department of Trade, it would not be held responsible for authorizing doubtful institutions. Lord Robens was also able to strengthen the banking expertise of the group by announcing the appointment of Mr E.B. Bennett, DSC, formerly chief of Exchange Control in the Bank of England, as a director.

The same report showed the earnings of the banking group, including bullion and base metal dealing, to be contributing nearly half the total JM profits. Surprisingly enough no breakdown of profits within the banking division was given; shareholders could not see how much of their profit came from bullion trading and how much from convential banking business. Even more oddly there was no separate balance sheet for the bank published in the report and accounts that went to shareholders. All was submerged in the results of a diversified commercial company; indeed the banking division as a whole occupied only one quarter page of a seven-page directors' report. Nor were any names of directors or officers of the bank shown, except that of the chairman, a company secretary, and the general manager, who had come to the post after twenty years in other parts of the group.

Two years later, as recorded in the report and accounts for 1982, the banking group continued to flourish, 'banking, dealing and trading' producing 48 per cent of all company profits, which were now increased to £49.6 million. It remained impossible to tell how much of this was derived from banking proper – the activities carried on by a conventional bank – but it is possible to piece together the probability of its continuing to be miniscule: of some 140 'principal products and services' offered by JM, four only were conventional banking activities. This impression was strengthened by the prose of the report: 'banking continued to make excellent progress and achieved a record profit for the year. The ability to deal in precious metals with customers in three of the world's most important markets, London, New York and Hong Kong, was a prime reason for this success, augmented by the planned and rapid expansion in general banking business ... ' Precious metal processing and trading, base metal trading and the acquisition of a broker dealing in 'soft' commodities – coffee, cocoa and sugar – are described in the report but banking proper is dealt with in a single clause: 'the planned and rapid expansion in general banking business where we specialize in the financing of international trade'.

That was that. Shareholders knew that somewhere in their company was a subdivision of a subsidiary engaged in financing international trade, but as to where, for what periods, in what quantities, to whom, and by whom, no hint was given. Shareholders might well assume that it was but of the slightest importance.

Their attention was instead focused on America where profits, which had represented 21 per cent in 1979, and 18 per cent in 1980, had grown to 27 in 1981 and 32 per cent in 1982. No division of these profits was shown, although it seems clear that a substantial part must have come from precious metal trading in New York, which produced 'really excellent figures'. It was in a different sector that investment was concentrated – manufacturing jewellery, for the expansion of which the paid-up capital of Johnson Matthey Investments Inc., the holding company, was increased from $59 to $96 million.

Surprisingly little information was given to shareholders even on the subject of these important investments. No details of past performance, management, or corporate structure of the companies acquired was given. Not even the amounts invested were shown, only a short statement: 'Acquisitions – The Group continued its policy of selective investment in new business and made the following acquisitions' (which included chemical manufacturing firms in France and Scotland, a research company in Wales, a pigment producer in Holland, a jeweller in New Zealand and four jewellery firms in the USA, one of which was the Catamore Company, 'one of the US's leading jewellery manufacturers and marketing companies', at a cost of £15 million).

The US jewellery investments started to go wrong with crushing suddenness; more probably, the cynic might say, they had been bad to start with. It was necessary, in the next annual report (1983), to state to shareholders that 'the most seriously affected business in North America was our jewellery operation. We were trying to build up a new business at a time when the market was depressed ... but we believe that, in the future, jewellery will offer a growing potential business for our group.' That year the Americas produced only 6 per cent of the profits, which as a whole dropped from £49.6 million before tax to £38 million.

Once again the shareholders were given no financial details of what had gone wrong and where.

But the next year they knew!

In the 1984 report and accounts the directors announced that the jewellery business, which had been acquired only two years previously, had consistently made losses, totalling over £17 million, from the date of their being acquired, and that it was to be sold at an estimated total loss of over £69 million.

No explanation of how these enormous losses were created was given in the annual report and accounts; Mr Lutley, who had been in charge of North America since 1980, resigned, although with the comfortable solace of a $400,000 payment. Shareholders licked their wounds, and were comforted by the promise that 'Trading losses ... will not recur. Further, providing our remaining US operations continue to trade profitably, the total rationalization costs would be offset by a saving of something close to £35 million in US corporate income taxes.'

At a time like this, when heads were rolling, boards of directors become agitated and distressed; the use of the word rationalization, which can mean either large-scale redundancies or the near avoidance of liquidation, is a symptom. Reading between the lines other indications of nervousness could be seen. It was decided to revalue the property of the group, which produced a surplus of £41 million, without which the assets would have taken a hard knock. As it was the directors stated that

> In view of the underlying profitability and as a result of the actions taken to offset the US jewellery write-off, shareholders' funds have increased in the year from £331.3 million at March 1983 to £351.4 million at March 1984. In addition our remaining base stocks were worth £43.8 million over book value.

The remuneration of the highest paid director was increased from

£63,000 to £73,000; four more directors joined the ranks of those earning over £60,000. These figures referred only to UK emoluments.

Two other statements were curiously juxtaposed; that made by the directors that 'In its general banking role JMB has reorganized and expanded its team of specialist personnel. As a result, this business has continued to grow at a rapid pace and on a broad base. Consequently the bank's share capital has been increased by £10 million to £60 million', and that of the chairman, now, following Lord Robens's retirement, H. R. Hewitt, 'It has also been deemed prudent to increase Johnson Matthey Bankers Ltd's provisions against loans outstanding. As a result the banking group's profits are well down from the record of the previous year.' No indication of the size of the provision was given. Nor, of course, of the loan book itself. The dividend, although uncovered, remained, and for the first time a statement of the banking group's net assets was given. This was, as a method of judging the health of the bank, nearly useless. So much of the balance sheet was held in metal stocks – £1,200 million from a total of £2,089 million – that an analysis of the banking assets was impossible. What could be seen should have been enough to sound a warning bell; stocks and debtors came to £1,995 million, creditors to £1,919 million, which is uncomfortable; only £22 million, or just over 1 per cent of total assets were in the form of cash and bank balances. Current, deposit and other accounts were lumped together under creditors. Without comparable figures for past years and a separation of the metals business no authoritative indication of the capital resource behind the banking business proper could be ascertained.

In spite of the board's brave words it was obvious that Johnson Matthey was having a tough time. All available stops had been pulled out, and there was little left to do in the way of window dressing, especially since jewellery losses continued. The 1985 director's report stated that 'The estimated cost of withdrawing from our US finished jewellery operations was written off as at 31.3.84. In the event, the estimate made at that time proved inadequate and further provisions of £16.5 million have had to be made in the year.' In all nearly £80 million had been lost on this affair, the responsibility for which has never been made clear.

Responsibility was rendered even more difficult to pin down due to another of Johnson Matthey's little oddities – its treatment of the status of directors. In 1980 there were six executive directors, Mr Hewitt, managing director, Mr Hughes, deputy managing director and chairman of the North American Group, Mr Varrall, chairman of the Central Finance group and the Banking group, Mr Dumenil, Mr Lovell, chairman of Johnson Matthey Metals, and Mr Pateman.

Mr Lutley was appointed to the board in that year, as was Mr Bennet from the Bank of England; although Mr Lutley had been with the group since 1958 and was president of the principal US subsidiary, both were described as non-executive.

The next year the divisional director of the Metals Division was appointed to be an executive director; Mr Varrall relinquished his executive duties, while remaining chairman of the bank. Mr Lutley, although now divisional director in charge of North America, remained non-executive. So did Mr R. G. Wheeler, who was appointed as a non-executive director in 1983, although he had been with the group since 1952 and divisional director of the bank since 1980.

Mr Lutley left after the American disaster in 1983. Mr Thorburn joined the board as financial controller and executive director.

Thus during the period when North American and banking losses were incurred, both these divisions had non-executive directors at their head. It is of course possible that non-executive in Johnson Matthey had something other than its usual meanings.

Given this state of affairs it seems that no effective control was exercised by the main board over banking activities. Indeed, it is much more likely that, after the massive losses experienced in North America, responsibility for which must be laid on the board collectively, pressure was put on the banking division to produce some profits somehow from somewhere, and quickly: after all, business was 'growing at a rapid pace and on a broad base'!

It does not appear that the management of the bank required much persuading to go all out for profits, but, even had circumstances been propitious, any banking ability was lacking. When JMB became an authorized bank in 1980 one of the more important criteria used by the Bank of England in assessing suitability was that of the experience of management. On paper this could hardly have been very convincing. The chairman of the banking group was Mr Paul Varrall, who had been company secretary of the parent company, had no practical experience of, nor qualification in, banking; the chairman of the parent company, Mr Hewitt, was a manufacturing chemist, who had learned his trade making soap and explosives.

Some comfort might have been, but clearly should not have been, drawn from the presence on the parent company's board of the Bank of England's former official, Mr Bennett.

Leaving aside the question of fraud, at present under investigation, the errors of JMB were commonplace. In the run up to 1984, under pressure to produce results, managers lent too much money to individual customers, and badly misjudged the character and standing of those customers, who were mainly Pakistani businessmen engaged in the most speculative of ventures. Such mistakes may take place in any bank, when management controls are lax and lending officers anxious, for reasons more or less creditable, to please. What distinguished JMB was the inordinate size of the exposures compared with the total assets of the bank and the fact that all the bank shares were controlled by a single conglomerate company with limited resources. Faced with similar circumstances a freestanding bank would have been able to cope by arranging standby credits and, if needed, calling upon management support from fellow banks.

Such a bank would also be in direct contact with the Bank of England. JMB was submerged in a division whose most important business was metal trading, along with futures broking and international insurance broking. Being part in turn of a group where the major contributor was a chemicals and refining business, the bank officials were clearly well down the pecking order. Nor, faced with severe inroads in their capital, was the parent group nearly large enough to absorb banking provisions.

When matters came to a head – and they continued to escape the attention of both Johnson Matthey's auditors and the Bank of England for a considerable time – the Bank stepped in with practised speed. On 1 October 1984 JMB were bought for £1 by the Bank of England: directors left and were replaced by Bank nominees; new management was provided; the clearers put up £75 million, the Bank £100 million towards reconstruction, and the police were called in later to investigate possible frauds.

A loan book of some £400 million, of which £310 million were classified as bad or doubtful, and provisions of £220 million indicated to be necessary, were revealed. Good management, combined with financial resources sufficient to soak up the losses, produced results, and is enabling the business to survive for either sale or an orderly liquidation. In the long run it is even possible that the whole of the extra cash provided might be recovered.

The Bank of England, although it failed in a supervisory role, proved itself as adept as ever at launching a lifeboat. It has, however, not been sufficiently realized to what extent JMB's difficulties were due to its position as a subsidiary of a non-banking conglomerate. Consider the position of the directors of the parent company who were not directors of the bank. They would be entitled only to the most general of reports; banking confidentiality would demand that a customer's affairs should not be disclosed outside the bank itself, and bank officials can become very regimental on the subject of confidentiality when they have something to hide. The same officials that had been responsible for making the dud loans would be reporting to the Bank of England. Under such circumstances, if a bank executive has something to hide, it is very easy for him to do so.

The lessons to be learnt seem clear:

(a) that banking business must be transacted and recorded absolutely separately from associated trading ventures;
(b) that only in the most exceptional circumstances should a bank be a subsidiary of a non-bank;
(c) that in all circumstances capital assets must be sufficient for a bank's business, without relying on the support of shareholders, unless these too are banks who have formally agreed to unlimited support;
(d) that the sufficiency of information given by a company to its shareholders should be ensured.

This last is a matter for the Stock Exchange.

Public awareness of Johnson Matthey's banking activities derived from the published annual reports and accounts, which regularly contained only the slightest information on these matters, was inevitably sparse, and, as events proved, also misleading.

The Stock Exchange, naturally enough, is reluctant to agree; the Bank is reluctant to criticize the Stock Exchange. Both unite in questioning the conduct of JMB's previous auditors, who are currently being sued for alleged negligence.

A more fundamental question can be raised: was the Bank of England right in its decision to bail out Johnson Matthey Bankers; or would it not have been better in the long run to insist that the parent company should bear the whole responsibility? The Bank has no doubt: its action was firmly in the tradition of Montagu Norman, and followed the successful precedent of the solution found to the secondary banking crisis ten years before.

There are however important distinctions to be made. The problems of JMB were unique, arising from what seemed extraordinary incompetence concealed both by the position of the bank as a wholly owned subsidiary and the unusual nature of its business, with bullion trading as a central part. In the secondary banking crisis the difficulties of the time – unprecedentedly high interest rates combined with high levels of borrowing on the wholesale market – affected the whole financial community.

The reason given at the time of the rescue was that the collapse of JMB would threaten the stability of the bullion market, but this explanation was not received with universal credulity. Even were it so, an alternative course, which would have been possible at no cost to the taxpayer, would have been to insist that the shareholders of Johnson Matthey plc assumed responsibility, with the assistance of their own bankers. As it was, the NatWest was dragooned, not without understandable peevishness, into supporting the rescue; its support might have been more enthusiastic if the Bank of England had adopted the course of providing a standby credit to

NatWest ensuring that the shareholders ultimately paid, rather than, in effect, going the whole hog of nationalizing JMB. As a result the shareholders of JM plc are doing very well indeed now the incubus has been removed; shares stand at 180p and on a price/earnings ratio in the twenties, indicating a fair degree of optimism. What is more, a potentially dangerous signal has been sent out: however small and scruffily managed a bank may be, so long as it is a 'proper' bank, the Bank of England will not allow it to fail.

In the context of the wildest outburst of activity by new and untried organizations the City of London has ever seen about to occur, this message will encourage ventures that should be very firmly repressed. Many other managers will shortly find themselves in the same position as those JMB executives who, pressed for results, took unwarranted risks.

PART THREE

In Another Country

'I too have committed fornication,
But 'twas in another country, and besides,
The wench is dead.'

MARLOW *The Jew of Malta*

9

Midland Crocker

'Clouds lingering yet, in solid bars
through the grey west ... '

Although it was the affairs of the smaller banks that prompted most concern in the 1970s more recent anxiety has focused on the difficulties of larger banks.

Grindlays was hit in the early years of the 1980s by a combination of shipping bad debts, losses in France, both of which were peculiar to itself, and the general concern over Latin American debts. While any one, or even two, of these would not have been too damaging, the combination was, and the takeover by the Australia and New Zealand Bank came as a salvation.

Almost all international banks had shared in the 1970s' lending boom, and suffered correspondingly in the 1980s. Levels of exposure varied considerably between the banks, with Midland among the British being seen to be most deeply involved in loans to Third-World countries of doubtful fiscal trustworthiness. Midland had a total Mexican exposure of £1.6 billion, not much less than the two biggest American banks (Citibank $2.9, Bank of America $2.86) and more than any of the others.

Attitudes towards the international debt problems vary considerably from inspissated gloom to relaxed confidence, depending very much on where one stands. Morgan Guaranty, for example, the epitome of solidity, has only $1.2 billion outstanding, a sum from their point of view entirely manageable. Elsewhere fingernails are often bitten down, and nowhere recently more so than in Midland Bank's Poultry headquarters.

When in 1985 Kit McMahon, the highly regarded Deputy Governor of the Bank of England, announced his intention of becoming chairman of the Midland, it was assumed that a solution to that bank's problems would soon be found, if indeed it had not already been discovered. True enough, the unhappy marriage and rapid divorce of the Midland and Crocker National banks has now been concluded. Crocker has taken up with another partner and Midland, heaving a sigh of relief, has abandoned its expensive foreign adventure; all done before Mr McMahon took up his new office.

The Midland Crocker liaison was contemporaneous with the Johnson Matthey affair, and shared some characteristics. Both JMB and Midland were authorized banks, although of very different size, and subjected to the minimum Bank of England supervision: both were driven by what they saw as the imperative of expansion, and both got it wrong.

While some uncomfortable passages must have been experienced, the Midland has rescued itself by its own exertions, without the intervention of the Bank of England, but has in doing so underlined some significant weaknesses in banking control.

Before the Reagan administration began dismantling some of those barriers to trade erected in the desperate days of the recession, an absurd situation existed: with little difficulty American banks were able to establish themselves in Britain, and even to open branches wherever they wished; indeed they might do so in many countries of the world, but in the US they were confined within the boundaries of their own home state. The Bank of America, the biggest bank in the world, had branches in most major French towns but could not open one anywhere in the US outside California, but the Midland Bank of Great Britain was free to buy out a large and competitive bank in California, or in any state it might choose; admittedly it was true that this could only be done after a good deal of negotiations with the Federal Reserve Board, the American banking authority, who were conscious not only of the problems raised by foreign control and their own limitations in coping with it, but sensible of the annoyance many US banks felt at what seemed to be, and indeed was, unfair discrimination. Participation by a foreign institution in a US bank was therefore made the object of searching enquiry and extensive negotiations with the US regulating agencies.

The enthusiasm with which the board of the Midland Bank announced, on completing such negotiations in 1980, its acquisition of 51 per cent of the share capital of the Crocker National Bank of California at a price which valued the whole at over $1.1 billion, was understandable and, apparently, justified. California, as its inhabitants are fond of reminding one, would be the sixth (or seventh depending on their degree of enthusiasm) economic power in the world, were it an independent sovereign state. The GDP of California had a faster growth rate than that of any other American state, nearly half as much again as the national average: its population was the richest, and the University of California was the finest in the world, with Nobel prizes coming thick and fast. Above all, Silicon valley, with thousands of companies of all sizes embodying diverse aspects of high technology, was indisputably the microchip capital of the world.

Crocker was the oldest national bank in California, dating from 1850, with a charter of 1870. Apart from the enormous Bank of America, it was one of the two largest in the state and the twelfth largest in the USA, with 382 branches serving a loan portfolio of $14 billion. Crocker's international division had offices in six Asian countries and Brazil, Venezuela and Mexico.

Midland's description of its new affiliate in the 1981 report and accounts approached the breathless:

> Crocker's performance over the ten years 1971 to 1980 has been most impressive. Net income increased from $36 million to $95 million representing a compound growth rate of 11.3 per cent. During the same period assets have grown by an average of 13 per cent annually and deposits by 12 per cent. Interest income grew at an even faster rate, 20.3 per cent, and this could have been greater . . .

A recent hiccup was admitted: Crocker's profits had fallen from $147 million to $68 million after bad debt provision of $85 million, but there was no suggestion that this was anything but a temporary setback arising 'primarily because its cost of funds increased more rapidly than its ability to charge those increases'. The optimism seemed to be justified as the following year brought a 31 per cent increase in Crocker profits: Crocker was also initiating new products, had opened one fully automated branch and another with solar-powered airconditioning, and moved into two new skyscraper headquarters, all in the best traditions of Californian expansionism. The prose of the Midland annual report was, however, muted, drawing attention to the longer-term benefits of what was still referred to as the Crocker alliance, although by this time the Midland held a decisive 57 per cent of the equity:

> We made the Crocker investment as part of a long-term plan for the international expansion of Midland Bank Group. After working together for just over a year, through the difficulties of a severe world recession – and the particular problems of the US banking industry – we are clear that the medium- and long-term benefits of the Crocker alliance will be substantial.

Latin American problems were singled out in an explanation of why group specific provisions had been increased from £113 to £196 million:

> As a major international banking group with a history of close relationships with overseas countries going back into the nineteenth century, it is inevitable that we should be faced with a number of situations in regard to our lending – South and Central America and in Eastern Europe, for example – where the restructuring of payments of both

interest and principal indicates the need to make some prudent provision against possible loss, although that loss may be by no means certain.

It is not possible to be in international banking business – as your Bank has been, profitably and successfully, for many years – without risk, however careful the assessment. It has to be remembered, too, that these international loans were, to a large extent, the counterpart of the huge recycling of surplus income from oil producers over the last decade. If the international banking community had not acted as the agent for these transfers, a very serious imbalance would have arisen in the world's monetary system, and international trade, including very substantial exports by our customers, would have been greatly impeded.

There was no suggestion however that any of this applied to Crocker. But next year the grim reality was undisguised. In the report and accounts published in March 1984 it was revealed that Crocker had found it necessary to make provisions of over $173 million, driving them into a loss:

The results of Crocker National Corporation since we acquired our 51 per cent holding in 1981 (later increased to 57 per cent, on a fully diluted basis) have been disappointing – particularly in the light of Crocker's results in the previous five years which, reflecting the enthusiasm of a new and vigorous management team and a buoyant Californian economy, showed a continuous upward trend.

The general effects of the world recession and the sharp reversal of California's exceptional growth rate, combined with the specific effects of exposure in real estate and agricultural loans, led to a position in which the total amount of Crocker's non-performing loans created a strong probability of a depressing effect on earnings for some years ahead. To give the necessary flexibility required to reduce the non-performing loan portfolio, the Crocker Board informed us in December 1983 that they had decided to set aside a special provision of US $107 million out of 1983 profits making a total provision for the year of US $173 million (£120 million). As a result Crocker reported a loss before tax of US $20 million in 1983.

The essential soundness of the investment – no longer given the status of an alliance – continued to be emphasized:

Our investment in Crocker was made as part of a long-term strategic development to broaden our international base. The events of recent months do not alter our view of the correctness of the strategy or our confidence that Crocker will in due course prove a sound and necessary investment.

Nor did the remedial action appear dramatic: the Crocker management were left in post, a Midland director being sent out to act as senior vice-president, and 'a number of steps ... taken to ensure that Midland Bank exercises a greater measure of control over its largest overseas investment'.

Much more interesting information was disclosed in an attached addendum to the report and accounts, entitled 'Supplementary Financial Information'. This was the result of a requirement of the US SEC following Midland's submission of a US loan prospectus, and was the first time that a UK bank had been required to submit such detail to its shareholders. There was no reason why this should not have been done many years before, apart from the near obsessive secrecy that characterizes so much of English life. Cogent reasons may be advanced why banks should be able to preserve confidentiality, but not to the extent of the fussy nannying that has been for many years the norm.

The supplementary information covered not only Crocker but the whole of the Midland group and among its nine pages was an analysis of risk elements in the group's loans. The SEC demands that loans already in difficulty, those potentially so, foreign outstandings, and loan concentrations, should be disclosed. Among the foreign outstandings three countries were shown as representing more than 1 per cent of total group assets.

Table 4

Country	£ billions outstandings	Percentage of gross assets
Brazil	1.3	2.4
Mexico	1.0	1.8
Argentina	0.6	1.1

A bank's assets are the total of its loans, investments, debtors, cash and fixed assets; at that time Midland's assets totalled £52.613 billion: shareholders funds, including reserves, were of course a much smaller figure – £1.9 billion.

Midland's problem advances, disclosed under SEC regulations, amounted to £1.3 billion of non-accrual, past due and restructured debt; some of this total related to foreign debt included in the table shown above.

Bankers will make the point that while these figures are arithmetically correct they contain no element of judgement and therefore appear unduly dramatic. Most of such loans are secured, and the question that must be asked, and can only be answered, by management is what sum it may be prudent to set aside in the light of their own knowledge of the status of the loans? The Midland management published their assessment of this as the provision in the accounts for bad and doubtful debts, which amounted at the end of 1983 to the not uncomfortable total of £673 million, or over 2 per cent of total lendings reserved against possible defaults.

But in twelve months even this substantial sum was seen to be inadequate when the 1984 results were produced, showing £534 million being written off as an inevitable loss. In addition another £616 million was brought into provisions for bad and doubtful debts, now increased to a total £849 million, or 2.2 per cent of total assets, very nearly the equivalent of half the parent company's capital.

It was Crocker that was to blame; the Californian bank had produced a staggering loss of £356 million, which they managed to reduce by £134 million after selling off one of their new skyscrapers. The Latin American exposure was shown to have further increased, with the three problem countries now absorbing 6.7 per cent of all the Midland group's loans.

Table 5

Country	£ billions outstanding	Percentage of total loans
Brazil	1.9	3.0
Mexico	1.6	2.5
Argentina	0.8	1.2

Midland Bank Accounts

Of these half the Argentine loans were now clearly in the problem category: $280 million-worth were Crocker loans.

Since such a state of things could hardly be allowed to continue, and decisive action was seen to be imperative, Midland bought out the minority to take full control of Crocker with a 100 per cent shareholding, and replaced the senior management. There was no more reference to Crockers being 'in due course a sound and necessary investment'.

There is perhaps nothing unusual in the sad story of Midland and Crocker except the sheer size of the misfortune. Bank takeovers are more difficult to plan and execute than those in an industrial company. The value of any bank lies in its assets, and since most of these consist of loans the evaluation of a bank becomes the evaluation of the loan book. It is difficult enough for a bank to rate its own book correctly, and impossible for another to do so. Even with the fullest co-operation from the bank to be acquired, which is rarely forthcoming, for a bank is reluctant to disclose too many of its secrets to another who may, should the bid not proceed, continue as a competitor, the time and effort involved in valuation is so great as to make it a practical impossibility.

Matters are different in a manufacturing company, the board of which, when an acquisition is mooted, can make a strategic study of what added strengths can be expected from access to new markets, research and development, production facilities and techniques. Premises, stock and tools can be accurately valued, debtors and creditors rated for quality, judgements made on key personnel. Information is readily obtainable from trade associations, suppliers and customers and may be supplemented by specialist consultants' reports. Even so, many mergers lead to unforeseen disappointments.

A smaller merchant bank may perhaps be sought out in order to secure the talents of some key personnel but, like bank loans, bank people are notoriously fungible. By procrastination and fumbling ANZ managed to lose almost all the best senior people in Grindlays within a year from the 1984 takeover. The personnel consideration is however only peripheral: in buying a bank one buys assets, and the only question should be what discount should be applied to them.

This the Midland did not, or could not, do in their purchase of Crocker. Spurred on by the difficulty of securing permissions, structuring the details of the deal itself and the sheer excitement, the questions of management, markets and above all the value of the loan book, took second place.

Given such a degree of uncertainty it is rare that any clear policy or precise objectives of management can be agreed. Flushed with success, describing their achievement in almost romantic terms ('the consummation' of 'an alliance'), a little dazed with the magnitude of it, boards tend to leave the management in post to get on with things; being especially prepared so to do when that management has made overoptimistic projections of performance which in time look progressively unrealistic.

Even the sale of Crocker to Wells Fargo in 1986 served to illustrate the pitfalls of international banking. Wells Fargo bought Crocker with the problems cleared out; Midland had previously taken over all Crocker's foreign loans, amounting to over $3 billion, which included all those difficult loans to South America. A provision was made against these at the time of transfer. The chairman did not mention this item in his report to shareholders, which was left to the review of group operations, but made the point that the price paid, £750 million, was the value of the Midland investment in Crocker shown in the bank's accounts, and represented 'a premium of some 25 per cent over Crocker's net tangible assets under US accounting principles'.

It really is rather odd that calculations of the assets of a large and important bank can differ by as much as 25 per cent when reported under different conventions. Since Wells Fargo, a bank distinguished by its toughness and realism, was presumably not paying for goodwill, it would suggest that the British standards might be more realistic than the American, which is a comforting thought for Midland shareholders.

With the disposal of Crocker bloodletting was stopped, although the question of problem loans remained. The adventure had been expensive; with nearly £1 billion being written off in three years shareholders' funds had been eaten into, reducing the strength of the parent company. It is difficult to see, however, that this is a failure of Bank of England supervision rather than a plain, but gross, Midland mistake.

Matters are complicated when a bank is bought by another operating under a different regulatory dispensation, and at a six-thousand-mile distance. Crocker management were responsible to Californian state and US authorities: the Bank of England had jurisdiction only over the parent company in London. Nor can a 400-branch $20 billion Californian bank be managed from London in any other than the most general way; decisions must be taken by those on the spot. Only at the time of purchase, or later to insist upon a sale, could the Bank of England intervene in any way beyond its normal monitoring.

The Midland was of course not the only British bank to lend more than it should have done to Latin America. The National Westminster Bank also found itself in 1983 having to report, under the same SEC rules as the Midland, an uncomfortable exposure to Mexico of £626 million, whichwas over 1 per cent of total assets: by 1984 this had risen to £795 million. Loans to Brazil had at the same time reached more than three quarters but less than 1 per cent of the bank's total assets. Total problem (non-accrual, past payment more than ninety days or 'troubled debt restructurings') loans totalled £1.137 billion, up from £1.022 billion.

A measure of the management's concern showed itself in a total year-end provision of £918 million, rather more than the £849 million set aside by the Midland even although National Westminster's problem loans were rather smaller, and had shown a much less steep rise in the past year. But provisions are made not only on grounds of what is prudent, but on what the balance sheet allows, for such international debt uncertainties place banks in a dilemma. It is customary to graduate outstanding loans in order of quality and certainty of repayment. Grade I might be those – it should be hoped the great majority – loans which were undoubted; normally advances to other banks and sovereign risks would be in this category. Grade II would be those where some irregularity, perhaps purely mechanical, existed, but where no real doubts were felt; as for example when a subsidiary of an undoubted parent had delayed payment on a local technicality.

Grade III would be problem loans, where delays in payment of interest, or repayment of capital, had been experienced, which required careful monitoring if they were not to slide into Grade IV, loans in real difficulty, where default on all or part was likely, or Grade V, which must be written off as irrecoverable.

In more equable times a prudent bank would consider it advisable to make provisions against loans it had graded between III and V, writing off for example 100 per cent of Grade V, 80 per cent of Grade IV and a third of Grade III, but with international problems on the present scale this can hardly be done. If it were banks would find themselves having to write off their entire capital. One British bank found that nearly 20 per cent of all loans were Grade III or below; making prudent provisions would have absorbed a sum equivalent to the bank's capital and reserves several times over.

The information that British banks have been obliged by US regulations to include in their reports to shareholders goes well beyond details of bad and doubtful debts.

The Midland Bank, for example, revealed in its 1984 report nine pages of supplementary financial information, such items as average interest rates and spreads on both domestic and international business of different types, and lending analysed by area and type of customer. This list shows that advances to UK manufacturing industry between 1980 and 1984 had risen only from £2,864 million to £3,595, while in the same period loans to the financial and services sector had gone from £2,987 to £5,335 million and personal loans from £1,647 to £4,635 million, a fact that tells us something about the continuingly static levels of investment in manufacturing in that interesting period.

Whether or not such information will continue to be given when the legal requirements cease is not yet known. The Bank of England is dubious, understandably but mistakenly. The dissemination of knowledge is therapeutic both to shareholders and management, for banks make their biggest mistakes when, realizing that a loan is going bad, they nevertheless choose to continue, fingers crossed, in the hope that matters may improve. If they are forced to reveal such difficulties executives are more likely to be able to brace themselves to make the necessary painful decisions. The fear of acknowledging that one has made an error and owning up is surprisingly prevalent even among senior bankers; one looks in vain, after some more than usually expensive mistake, for a candid acknowledgement that the board had got it wrong!

As a defensive mechanism an inter-bank trade in suspect loans developed from 1984. Although there was general agreement about value, different banks had different priorities, depending upon their country exposures and restrictions. Thus one bank might have an inconvenient amount of

Mexican debt falling due in 1987/8 which they would swap for a Peruvian debt, of lower quality, but a different maturity.

Rates for such transactions are kept fairly well under wraps, but one organization, the London banking analysis company IBCA, suggested that in October 1985 they were

Table 6

Country	Percentage of face value
Brazil	78–83
Mexico	78–82
Argentina	63–67
Venezuela	81–84
Chile	67–71
Peru	32–36

By early 1986 rates for Brazil and Argentina have hardened somewhat, while those for Mexico and Venezeula have fallen back, and the former significantly, as a result of falling oil prices.

IBCA also suggested that most large UK and US banks had so far reserved only against about 5 per cent of problem foreign debt, while French and German banks made provisions of up to 25 per cent, and Swiss banks well above this figure; they suggested that reserves should be made against at least 20 per cent of all problem loans, a figure in accordance with their assessment of major market discount.

Two problems stem from this. First, it is quite impossible for some banks to set aside this sort of provision; they simply do not have the resources to do so. Their strategy must be to ensure, if possible, rescheduling of the debt in such a way that at least the interest in paid, and they can preserve what often must be the fiction that some day they will recover their principal, even, it should be said, if it means lending more money to do so.

Other banks, with lesser exposures or greater reserves, will be much more inclined to walk away from rescheduling, taking their losses rather than, as IBCA puts it, to 'attempt sleight-of-hand accounting to put off the evil day'. It is this reason as much as any that makes a general agreement on international debt difficult, but in the absence of any such agreement the cloud continues to hang over all Western banks, and will signify its existence by the energetic efforts which will be made by these banks to strengthen their balance sheets by rights issues and unsecured borrowings.

10

International lending

'Mexico puts a strain on the temper.'

D.H. LAWRENCE

The difficulties experienced by the Midland Bank in Latin America were by no means unusual. By the end of 1985 Latin American external debt amounted to $368 billion; Mexico alone owed $97 billion abroad. About one third of this was owed by US banks, seven of which had exposures of more than $1 billion.

Table 7 USA bank loans to Mexico

	$ billion
Citibank	2.9
Bank of America	2.8
Manufacturers Hanover	2.0
Chase	1.7
Chemical Bank	1.4
Bankers Trust	1.3
Morgan Guaranty	1.2

Mexico is only a single example, albeit currently the most troublesome, of a much greater problem. Something like $1,000,000,000,000,000 (or a thousand billion dollars, which sounds less horrifying) is owed by poorer countries to richer. In order to keep up payments $100 billion or so each year are paid by poor countries to rich; and most poor countries want, and many in truth need, to go on borrowing more.

The trouble all began in October 1973, when the Arabs' third successive defeat at the hands of Israel made it clear to them that oil was potentially a more powerful weapon than any military one, as well as being a good deal more comfortable and less dangerous in use.

The subsequent success of OPEC (Organization of Petrol Exporting Countries) in raising the price of oil from $1.30 a barrel in 1970, to $2.70 in 1973, and, with another sharp rise after 1977, to $32.00 in 1981, changed the financial structure of the world. Since oil was paid for in dollars, a flood of this currency was swept into Arabian coffers. Of this golden shower only a proportion, in spite of the best efforts of many princelings, could be spent on palaces, yachts, motor cars, race horses and country houses in England and France, and in London casinos. Some might be, and in the more responsible states was, spent on infrastructure; airports, hotels, roads, housing, health and education, but not to great effect. Inevitably a great deal went on weaponry which, given the increasing complexity of armaments, is a wonderfully efficient method of soaking up spare cash, even in the absence of war.

All these desirable commodities could only be supplied by advanced industrialized countries, who proved successful in doing so to the extent that the initial balance of payments deficit experienced immediately following the first oil shock was soon converted into a credit. Poorer countries had little that could appeal to the newly rich Arab states and were unable to share in this counterbalancing trade.

Some, such as Pakistan, were able to provide labour to work on new Arab projects, and others, notably South Korea, developed heavy industrial plant which could be exported, but most had nothing to offer in exchange, and had to absorb the increased cost of oil as best they might.

While it was theoretically possible that this could have been done by decreasing domestic demand and increasing exports in an endeavour to balance the books, most Third-World countries lacked the political will to do so. Those that rode out the storm, and indeed prospered, were Asian: South Korea, Taiwan, Singapore, Hong Kong, and even India. The countries who could not, or would not, adapt themselves, were African and Latin American.

'To generalize', William Blake observed, 'is to be an idiot.' Bearing this firmly in mind, it is still difficult to avoid some generalizations about banking in the Third World, the less-developed economies, developing countries, or whatever euphemism is currently in fashion. It must be observed that some major Third-World countries observe the highest standards of probity and responsibility. In spite of the difficulties of being the largest, and one of the poorest, of the world's democracies, India's foreign debt remains one of the lowest: some $22.5 billion for a nation of 750 million. (Compare Brazil $102 billion [$73.76 to banks], population 130 million; Mexico $95.5 billion [$77.16 to banks], population 65 million.)

The proportion of Indian GNP applied to debt servicing stands at about 16 per cent: this is scheduled to rise to 20 per cent. International reserves are equivalent to nine months' imports. In 1984 India waived its right to the final instalment of an IMF loan. An honourable Civil Service does its best, under often difficult circumstances but usually successfully, to ensure that loans are debarred for improper purposes and used for their intended objects.

By contrast, both Zaire and Zambia, either of which could in reasonable hands be modestly prosperous, have external debts amounting to more than their entire GDP. While India's foreign borrowing has been put to economic use, this is not generally true of such debts in Africa. Bank loans are said to be fungible, that is, substitute uses may readily be found, and the funds diverted from their original purpose. Aid monies are even more fungible, as anyone who has visited Central Africa can report.

Expensive houses and motor cars for those in a position to benefit from what is in many countries almost universal corruption; presidential palaces, useless airports, foreign embassies, atomic power stations, steelworks (at one time it was fashionable for every African country to have a mini steelworks, running on non-existent scrap) and of course military personnel and equipment, took precedence over viable industrial and agricultural schemes. Even when funds were tied to such projects sheer incompetence took its heavy toll.

In Latin America things were done, as befits a more sophisticated society, on an even bigger scale. Just two countries – Brazil and Mexico – have run up more external debt than the whole of Africa: Venezuela, with 18 million inhabitants, has borrowed half as much again as India, with

Table 8 East Asian and Latin American economic performance

Country	Exports as % of GDP		Debt service ratio
	1965	1983	
S.Korea	9	37	90.1
Malaysia	44	54	16.9
Thailand	18	22	58.1
Indonesia	5	25	n.a.
Brazil	8	8	132.6
Argentina	8	13	214.9
Mexico	9	20	161.8
Venezuela	31	26	117.8
Peru	16	21	122.2
Chile	14	24	153.3
Weighted averages			
E.Asia	13	32	61.7
L. America	11	15	153.8

700 million. The preceding table (Brookings Institute 1985 Papers on Economic activity: J. Sachs) shows the increasing contrast between East Asian and Latin American countries. Starting from nearly the same proportion of exports as a percentage average of GDP in 1965, by 1983 East Asian countries were registering more than twice as high a figure as those in Latin America.

Unless, as was true of Venezuela and Mexico, debtor countries had oil of their own, they had no option but to increase borrowings in order to meet the new bills that came after the oil price rise. Obtaining loans did not prove difficult. The unspent oil revenues lay to hand, washing around in Western banks; the economies of those countries could only utilize a small proportion of the available funds for investment at home, although this was significantly more in some countries than in others. In the period 1970–78 14.4 per cent of the Japanese GDP was invested in domestic companies, 11.8 per cent as long-term borrowing; German companies got 7.3 per cent, of which 6 per cent was long-term; the UK 6.4 per cent, of which 3.3 per cent was long-term. (A rate of long-term industrial invest-ment running at less than a quarter of that of other countries is quite sufficient reason for any competitive failure in British industries.)

The banks were as willing as could be to lend the oil deposits on. After all, the loans were not to be made to private borrowers, who might go bankrupt, but to sovereign states, who had unlimited power. As Walter Wriston of Citibank said, 'Any country, however badly off, will "own" more that it "owes".' A state cannot go bankrupt: if it has short-term cash problems then an adjustment with its creditors, rescheduling repayments, will solve the problem.

Although the weakness of this hypothesis is now becoming clear, in the 1970s sovereign risk was king. In the years between 1972 and 1976 most major American banks doubled the proportion of their earnings from foreign lending: British banks could not have been far behind.

The business of lending devolved on bright young men in the international departments. With a bit of luck they might speak some Spanish, but very few had a word of Portuguese. This was hardly a barrier; as soon as their feet touched the ground of the country they visited, the bankers were whisked off to be entertained, flattered, provided with suitable companionship of the opposite sex, shown one or two impressive-looking projects, and returned home full of confidence in the great future of such a spendidly appreciative nation to which millions of dollars could be very profitably lent.

Should the sums needed be too large, a syndication could be arranged, with handsome front-end fees for all, especially the lead banks. Their successes were recorded in tombstone advertisements in the leading financial journals, reproductions of the same displayed in the international division's offices and photographs of signing ceremonies (with understandably happy borrowers) reproduced in the banks' house journals.

Putting together such borrowers and such lenders was to give an alcoholic a job as barman. Boards in London and New York purred with success as they saw the debts accumulate. Banks, like the Midland, who felt left out of foreign markets made every effort to buy other banks already in the happy position of having large Third-World portfolios.

For some time the process continued smoothly enough. The growth rate of the non-oil developing countries maintained a respectable annual average of 5.1 per cent, in the period 1973–81, after 5.8 per cent in 1967–72, before the oil rise, at a time when the industrialized countries' growth showed a decline from 4.4 to 2.8 per cent. But like the little bears in the poem the good governments got better and the bad got worse. It made little difference to the banks, who sat happily back and collected their interest as funds flowed out: in only the last four years Latin America has transferred more than $106 billion to industrial countries; more than twice the relative burden of German war reparations in the 1920s.

But nemesis was at hand. Almost all the commercial loans were made on a floating rate basis, a fixed margin being made on a base interest that reflected movement in the domestic lending rate of the currency employed, usually the US dollar, or the London interbank offered rate. From 1976, pursuing an anti-inflation policy, US domestic rates rose, and have since stayed at high levels. The cost of servicing dollar loans escalated accordingly. In the following year oil prices rose sharply again, from $13 a barrel to as much as $32, in 1981, more than doubling the oil import bill. The weaker economies, finding themselves now quite unable to keep up with the payments of interest and capital to which they were committed, began to go to the wall. The process of debt rescheduling began with the weakest, Zaire. Surprisingly, Poland was also in trouble: surprisingly because many Western banks had always regarded Eastern and European countries as particularly sound, since it was thought that however shaky their economies, Russia would always be at hand to bale them out. This proved not to be so.

Bankers do not usually object to rescheduling, regarding it rather as a phase through which countries go, rather like undergraduates having their debts paid by firm but generous parents. Developing economies are supposed to see the light, promise to amend their ways and do as a wise IMF tells them as a step on the way to financial maturity. Only the banks do not actually forgo the debts, of course; they merely agree to collect at a later date, and charge an extra fee for doing so. Meanwhile the interest is expected to keep flowing.

A typical deal might be that struck with Uruguay early in 1986 when repayment of a $2.6 billion loan, falling due between 1986 and 1989 (which was itself a rescheduling of a previous rescheduling) was postponed to 1988–96. The rate levied was one and three eighths over Eurodollar base, a very respectable spread for a sovereign loan, while part of the rescheduling which had previously been rescheduled was allocated an extra quarter per cent. Uruguay was also given a bonne-bouche by way of a small $44 million hydroelectric loan with World Bank participation.

This modestly successful package for one of the less troublesome countries involved thirty commercial banks; all of these as a result were able to continue carrying their Uruguay advances at full face value and to take the interest to profit. Come 1988, when the re-rescheduled debts fall due, the same process might well be repeated.

More recently, however, as debtors have been flexing their muscles, the compromises have become less advantageous to the creditors.

When President García of Peru in 1984 unilaterally announced a limit to what he was prepared to pay, and challenged the IMF's standards, the pattern was changed, and it is now the debtor countries who find themselves in a position where, if they cannot dictate changed terms, they certainly feel able not to have terms dictated to them. Brazil is going some way to following Peru's example, refusing to follow orthodox IMF policy and instead passing a budget that increased company and high earners' taxation while exempting the lower paid, and reducing the public deficit by only half of what the IMF had wanted.

Brazil worries banks, especially American banks, less than Mexico. Somehow or other Brazil will manage, but Mexico is nearer both disaster and the United States. In August 1982 Mexico had its first financial crisis and announced an immediate moratorium on its foreign debt, having borrowed $6.4 million in the preceding six months. There was no alternative for the banks but to agree to forgo the immediately due payments and create a rescue package involving an extra 7 per cent of new money, 'involuntary lending' from the banks, oil purchases by the USA, and IMF assistance. It seemed that this would be successful: a drastic austerity programme was initiated by President de la Madrid's government in 1983–4, public sector spending was slashed, the import bill was cut, inflation dropped, and as a result the economy showed a growth of 4 per cent in 1984. But 1985 brought presidential elections and the need to bribe the electorate, regarded in Mexico as inevitable. A mini boom was conjured up, and the ruling party allowed to 'adjust' the election with more than usual blatancy. The Mexico City earthquake, which was of great financial cost, estimated at as much as $16 billion, as well as cost in human suffering, made things worse, and the collapse of the oil price on which Mexican exports depended put the finishing touches.

Mexico was left at the beginning of 1986 owing nearly $100 billion, inflation mounting towards 80 per cent, capital leaving the country at the rate of $2.5 billion a year, with no prospect of doing much more than paying interest, which was running at 50 per cent of total export income, and urgently requiring large sums of new money. There was no prospect of Mexican workers, impatient at the rottenness and corruption of their system, agreeing to another austerity programme, so the whole problem was presented, in as polite a fashion as possible, to the American government.

Mexico is certainly looked on as being very much the USA's baby. With a common land frontier incapable of control and millions of Mexicans entering the US illegally, it is almost a subdivision of the US economy. Given the hysteria with which a Marxist government a thousand miles away in Nicaragua is received by some US politicians, the vigour of a reaction to anything so close to home as Ciudad Juárez can hardly be imagined.

With potential losses of such magnitude in prospect it might seem surprising that those involved did not go around quivering with agitation. There are at least three good reasons for this, as far as English banks go. First, and this applies to bankers of all countries and periods, a calm confidence must be seen to prevail. However dismal the prospects may be they can only be rendered worse by anything other than a display of unfaltering serenity.

Second, and giving force to this attitude, there is a lot of underlying security in international debt. Private persons may abscond and companies default, but countries only rarely refuse to pay their due debts; although often not in due time.

In the bad old days, before the Second World War, when international finance was much less well regulated, this was less true. Bondholders of Imperial Russian and Chinese issues are still waiting for their money, as indeed are those of the State of Missouri, which failed in 1841 and has not coughed up since. An absolute refusal to honour debts makes it difficult to borrow more, and unless governments are prepared to cut themselves off root and branch from world markets, as Burma did for many years, they accept the obligations of their predecessors. Besides, revolutionary changes of government are today the rule, rather than the exception, in many parts of the contemporary world.

The defaults of the 1930s bore primarily upon individuals. In a wave of indiscriminate selling American banks in the 1920s unloaded upon a gullible public South American bonds which rapidly collapsed to a minimal value. Individuals suffered, but banks, and bank directors, did very nicely indeed, and the ensuing scandal led to the establishment of the SEC.

The debts of the 1980s are not usually bonds held by persons but loans, owed to banks directly. Since there is no official market in these loans each bank may decide for itself what value should be attached to them in that bank's accounts: if there is an official market there is no choice in the matter.

Banks usually prefer to come to some arrangement that allows them to hold loans at their face value, while making whatever provisions they feel able against possible ultimate loss.

Restructuring debt is therefore the rule. This is of major importance, especially to US banks, for if interest is not paid within a specified time of the due date, provisions must be applied and suspensions made which directly affect profit. It is the effect on profit rather than capital that is significant. If, for example, the Midland Bank was to decide to provide against its Mexican debt a sum sufficient to reduce it to the current value in the market it would probably cost about £350 million, a sum equivalent to pre-tax profits. This would distress shareholders, and cause some embarrassment to directors (but bankers are not easily embarrassed), but have no other effect on net assets. Furthermore, the 1985 profit was stated after taking a charge against bad and doubtful debts of £431 million, which must have included a substantial element of Mexican risk.

Thirdly, after the Bank of England rescue of the small and badly run Johnson Matthey Bankers, it is widely assumed that any British bank can look to the Bank of England as a lender of last resort and picker up of the pieces. And, as the Bank of England themselves admit, even a Conservative government would nationalize an ailing clearing bank.

American banks do not have such comforting thoughts. Especially since depositors are protected by insurance schemes, as they have been to a modest extent in the US since 1979, US authorities are prepared to let quite a large bank fail. United American Bank of Tennessee, which collapsed in 1982, did so with total assets of over £2 billion. But Continental Illinois, an even bigger institution, was plucked from the rocks, and the largest banks could hope for a similar lifeboat to be launched.

The prospect is, however, quite sufficiently nasty to encourage bankers to put as much pressure as is seemly upon their governments to pull as many of their irons as convenient out of the fire. Dark hints are dropped to Treasuries about the potential disasters that might follow a unilateral debt renunciation on anything other than the smallest of scales. Given a period of stability, bank balance sheets could be strengthened so as to start once more expanding their international loan books, but this is simply not going to happen.

In the first place a period of stability is highly unlikely. Loans, which have hitherto been unquestioned, are beginning to look decidedly shaky. British banks with large exposures in Arab countries are starting to be querulous and uneasy when debtors appear to treat only the principal on loans as being repayable, protesting that the payment of interest is un–Islamic. In Abu Dhabi, debtors are suing for the return of interest they have already paid. Saudi Arabian courts have already reduced perfectly proper debts to negligible amounts by such methods. After some years of greedy spinelessness, when hundreds of millions have been lent to gentlemen whose intention to repay was always clearly of the vaguest (Grindlays was caught by a number), banks are becoming prepared to take firm action; although their prospect of success under the law available is not striking.

US banks also feel threatened by property wars in California and energy loans in the South West. More than \$60 billion of gas loans is outstanding; of this nearly 8% is already (March 1986) classified as doubtful. One senior banker was quoted as saying that there was 'at least a possibility that the shock to parts of our economic system could be so severe as to precipitate a crisis'. This judgement was made when oil prices were dropping towards \$13.50 a barrel: if the slump continues the crisis becomes closer. Failures in both these areas are inevitable.

With such dangers looming the situation is aggravated by the demands central banks are beginning to make on reporting banks' balance sheets, requiring that risk associated with items previously regarded as off–balance sheet be taken into account in capital ratios. Such requirements reduce even further those banks' ability to lend.

Government assistance is therefore essential. This may be channelled through the World Bank (if that institution is allowed to increase its capital sufficiently), but even the World Bank cannot provide a solution on its own. Harold Lever and Christopher Hulme, in their book '*Debts and Danger: the World Financial Crisis*', written before the drop in oil prices exacerbated matters so that the magnitude of the difficulties is underestimated, suggest that if existing lending is underpinned by governments guaranteeing that portion of their own banks' loans relating to approved debt, the banks would be able to resume new lending.

This proposal is analogous to what is already covered by Export Guarantee institutions, and authorities such as the Credit National in France, and was indeed put forward by me some ten years ago in relation to the extension of credits to British industry. I am therefore naturally convinced of its wisdom!

Without some such action it is only a matter of time before this chronic disease enters upon an acute and possibly terminal phase. When this happens even the Bank of England will find its skills of resuscitation stretched.

PART FOUR

The Magdalene of Lime Street

I I

Lloyd's

'Lloyd's coffee house has ever since been an empire of
almost incalculable resources.'

OBITUARY OF J. J. ANGERSTEIN

While the clearing banks were stirring in their sleep, troubled by monopolies and mergers, 123-banks, disappearing deposits, recalcitrant staff,
and new concepts of marketing, some difficulties were appearing to the
east of Leadenhall Market.

Lloyd's have always seemed, if understandably, to be a bit too pleased
with themselves. The oldest and by far the most glamorous institution in
the City, with memories of Nelson, Patriotic Fund swords, the Lutine Bell,
the Titanic, 100 A1 at Lloyd's, jostling in some confusion in the public
mind, Lloyd's of London is an international legend. Only the Bank of
England begins to compete in general esteem.

A fascinating odour of money hangs over the place: unlike a clearing
bank, staffed by only moderately prosperous wage-earners, and with
boards representing experience and virtue rather than wealth, the Lloyd's
market is composed of entrepreneurs, some of them very rich indeed and
all with the possibility of so becoming. Merchant banks, especially those
still controlled by the founding families, have directors with considerable
private fortunes, but they are few in number, and their institutions very
much smaller. Besides, merchant bank money is deployed discreetly:
Lloyd's flaunt it with Metro-Goldwyn-Mayer enthusiasm, reflected in
their architectural taste: the old Lloyd's building had more than a feel of
the Essoldo Cinema about it, but the new Rogers edifice is pure Star Wars.

But even opponents of the City and all its works are disarmed, at least
in part, by the thought that all these wealthy fellows have unlimited
liability, and can at any time lose everything down to the proverbial gold
cuff links. It is the sort of gamble that the English approve of; and Lloyd's
is a very English institution: while most banks were founded by Scots,
Welsh, Germans, Huguenots, or Jews, with some Quakers, the great names
at Lloyd's have been solidly middle-English, and the atmosphere remains.
(An exception should be made of John Julius Angerstein, the greatest of

91

them all, but it is the exception that proves the rule.)

Until very recently Lloyd's enjoyed a good press. Paul Ferris could comment, in terms of not-altogether-naïve enthusiasm, on 'a potent, clever, honest, successful ... the tremendous social kudos that goes with the membership of Lloyd's. It establishes a man's financial integrity, and provides a passport to practically every exclusive club in London.'

Such high regard did not endure for long, and only shortly after this was written in 1959 Lloyd's started going through a bad patch; 1965 was the worst year for claims ever experienced: aggravated by Hurricane Betsy in the US the total loss was higher than any previous year's profits had been. With the increasing sophistication and the consequent cost of aircraft and ships, to say nothing of inflation, much higher amounts of cover were required, but at just the time when more capacity was vital, members, discouraged by unexpected losses, were resigning at a remarkable rate. From 1966 the number of resignations doubled: in 1968, which was the 1965 result year, an unprecedented 148 names resigned, more than in the seven years before 1965.

The society was worried, and took action. Like any committee, the elected committee of Lloyd's, which ran the affairs of the corporation on behalf of its members, is no stranger to criticism, and much of what it did, and more importantly did not do, has been the subject of justified objection, but it should be acknowledged that the step it took in 1968 was bold enough. The committee asked Lord Cromer to chair a working party to examine the future of Lloyd's. Such a step is tantamount to agreeing the recommendations in advance: a Royal Commission's recommendations may be politely disregarded, but those of a committee headed by so powerful a man as Lord Cromer must be heeded. That, at least, was the theory: in fact the report was never published in its entirety, and some proposals, the acceptance of which could have avoided some unhappy events, have still to see the light of day.

On the central issue the results of the Cromer report fulfilled all expectations; underwriting capacity was increased by widening the limits of acceptability for new names and raising premium limits.

Since that time membership has continued to rise from something over 5,000 to more than 27,000. Now far removed from Boodle's, Lloyd's might be more aptly compared with the RAC. The Cromer committee recommendations on capacity expansion were welcomed and great efforts made, probably too great, to recruit new members. Introductory commissions are paid to those who introduce names: a class of 'mini members' who need only show wealth of £37,500 has been created; the insistence of British citizenship has been dropped: the interview by the committee has become a formality in so far as any vetting of the member goes, its prime purpose being to ensure that the candidate fully comprehends the liabilities he may incur.

Pre-Cromer underwriting members were mostly either engaged in the market itself, or closely connected to it. The expansion has brought new and critical people into Lloyd's; people who are concerned to monitor the safety of their underwriting, and not willing to leave it all in the hands of the professionals, people who, believing themselves to have been robbed, are not content that the matter should be swept under the carpet in the cause of preserving the reputation of the corporation; and who perhaps, not being active in the market, do not understand as clearly as those who are, the vital importance of maintaining its freedom and reputation.

Since there is much confusion, not confined to the Labour Party, it is worth while outlining how Lloyd's works. It is not a company: it has been aptly defined as a worker's co-operative, the oldest and biggest in the world. (Defined by me, though Peter Miller, the chairman of Lloyd's, while wholeheartedly approving of co-operatives, suggested that this description conveyed an inaccurate sense of mutuality. As the committee on behalf of the members is assuming increasing responsibility for righting wrongs and compensating unjustly treated members, the force of this objection seems to me to be weakened: but it is an interesting debate.)

Policies written by an insurance company are backed by the capital and reserves of the company; Lloyd's policies rely in the first instance upon the assets deposited by names and secondarily by the unlimited liability assumed by them; its capacity is limited by the number of those names, who are not acting as investors. They assume a more fundamental commitment by the acceptance of unlimited liability, which is explained to everyone before joining in a clear and distinct fashion. Names know what it is they are letting themselves in for, and do not therefore require the same level of protection as investors who may be sold a pup by share pushers or insurance salesmen.

Lloyd's is above all a market-place, as much as Covent Garden or Billingsgate, buying and selling risk rather than fruit or fish. It has the visible stalls which contain characters every bit as much picturesque as any Smithfield bummaree. It is not a conformist place: eccentricity is not only tolerated but welcomed. Like all markets, Lloyd's loves gossip. Tales are still lovingly told of the underwriter who never actually sat in the box, but wrote all his slips of the top of his hat, one leg perched on the seat, and changing legs at regular intervals: and he who, ceasing work promptly at three every day, devoted the next thirty minutes to sexual congress with his secretary.

Each class of participant has developed characteristic traits. Post-Cromer, when the overwhelming majority of capacity depends upon external names, their affairs are handled by a members' agent or, more correctly, underwriting agent, who must be the soul of tact and discretion. He is responsible for recruiting names, explaining the system to them and choosing syndicates for them. Well-established agents have links with the best syndicates, participation in which is much sought after, and which can pick and choose their names. Lesser agents do as best they may, but often have to fill up their member's capacity with new and unproved underwriters or have them write less than their limit. Not that the standing of a syndicate is necessarily any guarantee of prosperity: PCW was one of the best known and most highly regarded – and for years one of the most successful – underwriting names on the market. Names were queuing up to join until the very day the scandal broke.

To the members' agent falls the pleasant task of dispatching the yearly cheque, or the less pleasant one of making a demand for cash. Now that all syndicates publish their results names can see where they stand in the league table, and congratulate or censure their agent accordingly. The agent takes a fee and a commission for his services, his only risk being the uncertainty as to the size of the commission. Any successful members' agent has all the qualities that would embellish any embassy, and stands in constant need of them. Members' agents are often owned by brokers, and a possible conflict of interest may arise, which is being examined by Sir Patrick Neill's committee. In practice, agents are fiercely loyal to their names, a loyalty not weakened by the fact that their remuneration is linked to the profitability of those names. Members' agents share with the underwriters both the basic fixed commission, and a proportion of the profits.

Brokers are the giants of Lloyd's: the ten biggest are all public companies with commission incomes of over £50 million. Not all of this, by any means, goes to Lloyd's, for while all business must be introduced to Lloyd's by a Lloyd's broker there is no compulsion on him to place his risks with Lloyd's. Indeed probably three quarters of total premium income is placed with other insurers, mainly the companies.

Brokers are salesmen, and have salesmen's qualities and vices. They sell cover to their clients, and their clients' risk to underwriters, and depend for their well-being (a subject particularly dear to brokers' hearts) on the volume of business they can put through. The temptations are obvious: to sell the client cover he does not need, and to gloss over the risks when placing with an underwriter. In their Lloyd's business these temptations are usually successfully avoided.

In the first place most of the hard sell insurance is in the life market, where individuals are persuaded to take cover which they may or may not need on terms which may well not be the most advantageous to them.

Lloyd's is not involved in this market. And while a broker may 'pick up' a victim, as the Lloyd's expression has it, once, he is unlikely to succeed twice. Pale and disconsolate figures can be seen in the Room, who, their virginity being lost, find themselves shunned by many underwriters, and are driven to place their business where they may.

It is chastening to consider the sheer volume of sales talent employed by British brokers: in their highly competitive world the best are unequalled. If a fraction of the effort could be redeployed into industry this country's economic prospects would be bright indeed. But brokers can earn their £100,000 a year at an age when a sales director in industry is lucky to see a quarter of this, and Lloyd's can take their pick of talent.

They also earn it in an enviable way: business can be and is done at racecourses, nightclubs, villas on the Côte d'Azur, yachts, and in varying other places of resort, all more desirable than a motel in Wolverhampton. Since so much of their business is placed outside Lloyd's, brokers are to that extent outsiders. It has been rare for a practising broker to be elected to the chair of the committee. Living in a fiercely competitive world some brokers have rather more flexible ethical standards than would be acceptable in the market: the payment of commissions to clients' insurance managers, for example, is by no means unknown.

Underwriters are the core of Lloyd's. Forming the production line, the present managing agents of syndicates are the descendants of those underwriters who sat in their boxes in the Room and accepted risks for one account alone. Today they manage the affairs of a number of syndicates which might in turn comprise more than a thousand names in each. Managing agents, compared with brokers, are small, only two are public companies – but it is on their ability to assess risk that the prosperity of the whole market rests. They are a diverse crew, containing men of great intellectual capacity and others who appear to be 'idiots savants', their sole but golden ability being that of accepting good risks while avoiding bad. Hubris may beset the successful: Ian Posgate was the most remarkable figure seen in Lloyd's in recent years. His names were, and for the most part remain, faithful followers, for not only did he produce substantial profits year in and year out, but these were handed over to his names at the very beginning of the accounting year, five months before any other syndicate paid out.

Lloyd's is properly proud of the reputation of its underwriting: no policy holder has ever suffered by any defalcation on the part of underwriters, and the consequent value of a Lloyd's policy is proverbial.

Any market, even one as well established as Lloyd's, can be troubled by dishonest traders, and needs policing against them. Concurrently with the expansion of underwriting capacity, and probably to some extent because of the large and tempting sums now involved, a rash of frauds came to light in the 1980s. Some of these were not unprecedented, for insurance fraud is omnipossible; underwriters cynically but accurately assume that a percentage of claims are bound to be fraudulent; unless they can prove that this is so they must still pay up, and do so. The *Savonita* case was one such in which fraud was alleged; what distinguished it was not that some Italians were thought to have been engaged in the time-honoured activity of claiming for non-existent damage (although all those accused were eventually acquitted by an Italian Court), but that someone made a fuss about it. The committee of Lloyd's, in equally time-honoured manner, attempted to keep the whole matter from the public eye and after some delay produced a report remarkable for its tendentiousness: 'a shoddy document that smacks heavily of kangaroo justice', observed *The Economist*. 'The way in which Lloyd's ... has mishandled the *Savonita* affair has dealt its reputation the worst blow in living memory. Not to put too fine a point on it, it has succeeded in making itself appear both incompetent and somewhat cowardly', the *Sunday Times* commented in 1979.

Lloyd's did not appear to much greater advantage in the Sasse scandal. This resulted from careless and incompetent underwriting culminating in numerous calls being made on the names. Although counting among them the most eminent and respectable personages, well acquainted with the doctrine of unlimited liability and in no way reluctant to meet their obligations, this seemed too much. The names took legal action and forced a settlement from a reluctant committee, who had to pay some £16 million from corporation funds, which did not make them popular with the other members of Lloyd's.

Neither of these cases resembles the later Lloyd's scandals – centring round Howden and PCW. Incidents of the *Savonita* type are too common to warrant undue fuss. Any loss adjuster could produce dozens of examples of cases in which underwriters, rather than incur time and expense in the investigation of questionable claims, prefer to pay up and have done with it.

Nor is mishandling of syndicates' affairs uncommon. Names must take the rough with the smooth and vote with their feet. It was the high profile of both Sasse and some of his names that forced the issue into public attention, and it was the publicity that did the damage.

In no instance was there any question that policy holders might be placed at risk, always the question that worries Lloyd's, whose reputation is firmly and justly based on the fact that 'Lloyd's always pays'. It was either coincidence, or a common sharpening of expectations in the financial world, that produced at the same time the Gower report on investor protection, which addressed itself to a very different problem, the sale of securities and insurance to the public.

Lloyd's response to the *Savonita* and Sasse affairs in 1979, two years before Professor Laurence Gower was asked by the government to produce his study, was to form a working party under the chairmanship of Sir Henry Fisher, who combined experience as a don, a barrister, and in both the High Court and in the City. The Fisher report, published in May 1980, was precise, wide in scope and fudged no issues. Lloyd's could be seen to be setting its house in order, and doing so with some vigour. One issue was, however, not addressed. The Fisher committee was appointed to inquire into self-regulation at Lloyd's and for the purpose of such inquiry to review:

1) The constitution of Lloyd's (as provided for in Lloyd's Acts and Bye-Laws);
2) the powers of the committee and the exercise thereof; and
3) such working matters which, in the opinion of the working party, are relevant to the inquiry.

Its terms of reference did not permit it to discuss alternatives to self-regulation, which can hardly have been much of an inhibition, since the report, circulated, very wisely, to all members, stated: 'we have no doubt that Lloyd's will be best served by a properly conducted system of self-regulation. Indeed we do not see how it could function in anything like its present form under any other system of regulation.' A statement perhaps dubious, since it quite begs the question of whether the regulation of Lloyd's *should* indeed continue in its present form; the evidence at that time might be thought to be pointing in a contrary direction.

Within these limits, however, the Fisher report proved both sound and generally acceptable, forming the basis of the new Lloyd's Bill that was presented to Parliament in 1981. Not without some controversy within Lloyd's, especially on the proviso that brokers must divest themselves of their holdings in managing agencies, the Bill became law, a fact on which Lloyd's have been congratulating themselves ever since, for immediately after the passage of the Act a new wave of scandals broke which, in the absence of a self-regulatory statute, would have led to demands for compulsory external regulation which must have proved irresistible.

The timing of these events is relevant. The *Savonita* affair became public knowledge in 1978, when a debate in the House of Commons led to the formation of the working party, the report of which was published in September. The Sasse names challenged the committee in the summer of the following year. In January 1979 the Fisher committee was established; it reported in May 1980, and its recommendations were overwhelmingly (13,219 to 57) accepted by members in November.

But as far back as 1977 Ian Findlay and Bruce Gray, the deputy chairmen at that time, had realized that effective discipline was impossible under the constitution of Lloyd's as it was, and intitiated the chain of events that led to the passage of the Lloyd's Act on 23 July 1982. Their action started a full five years before anyone was aware of the scandalous behaviour that led to the current bitter disputes. The first of these, the Howden Group problems, surfaced in September 1982, and the misdoings of PCW the following month, although the origins of both went much further back, well before the Fisher committee, the first irregularities having taken place in 1970.

It is not easy to find fault with the 1982 Act. Under it the committee, composed entirely of working members, rarely skilled in the affairs of a large business, anxious above all, in what they believed to be the interests of the market and to maintain public confidence, to sweep scandal and discontent to oblivion rather than to maintain the principles of natural justice, and burdened by the outdated Act of 1871 that made effective discipline in any case difficult, resigned its powers to a new council, an elected body with power to manage the business of the society and to regulate the way in which members trade. Lloyd's external names elected eight members, working members sixteen, with four non-members co-opted by the council with the approval of the Bank of England. The council was given powers to pass by-laws which would have statutory force if approved by a majority of both working and other members. A disciplinary committee consisting of non-council members was given, subject to ratification by the council, wide powers of punishment, including expulsion. Previously this had only been possible if a vote of 80 per cent of all members had been obtained, clearly a near impossibility.

The new council of Lloyd's was accompanied by a new man in a new post. Ian Hay Davison, a senior partner of Arthur Andersen, was appointed, at the instigation of the Governor of the Bank of England, as chief executive.

Ian Davison is one of the ablest and most energetic, but not the most tactful or emollient of men. His task was not made easier by the lack of definition of boundaries between the chairman and chief executive, since both were full-time posts. In part the appointment worked well; there could be no doubt of the chief executive's dedication to enunciating new rules and ensuring that they bit. Outside names could be confident that the professionals would not easily again be able to sweep unpleasantnesses under the corporation's carpet.

But Davison was not so successful in his relationships with the committee or council. There were administrative untidinesses and clashes with the new chairman, Peter Miller, very much a professional Lloyd's man, which led to the chief executive's premature resignation and replacement. Without his initial fierce dedication to making a clean sweep, which could not fail to impress Lloyd's critics, it is likely that public opinion would have demanded, as fresh cases came to light, more stringent government action. As it was, a committee chaired by Sir Kenneth Berrill of the SIB recommended in 1986 only that the administrative machine should be overhauled.

The scandals that broke after the Lloyd's Act were different in nature from those that had engendered the Fisher committee and the Act itself. They did not present any danger of policy holders not being paid, but were quite simply the result of underwriters misappropriating funds.

The first to come to light was when the Alexander Howden Group, having been sold to an American company, Alexander and Alexander, was found to have some $25 million missing, presumably at the hands of the principals, Ron Comery and Ken Grob: from the investigation into this it was discovered that two underwriting agencies PCW and WMD Underwriting Agencies Ltd, both owned by a major Lloyd's broker and public company, Minet Holdings, had also made off with $40 million of their names' resources.

The ensuing investigations and disciplinary action carried out by Lloyd's unearthed the destination of most of this. A noted figure in the City, one John Wallrock, formerly chairman of Minets, admitted to taking £1.3 million as a secret share in a reinsurance programme with the PCW syndicates. Mr Wallrock has been expelled from Lloyd's and fined £500,000, a sentence against which he made an unsuccessful appeal.

Peter Cameron-Webb of the eponymous PCW did his 'dishonest misappropriation', as the disciplinary committee puts it, on a larger scale: he took £6.5 million, spending it on yachts, aeroplanes and other accessories to gracious living. His deputy, Peter Dixon, did even better, taking over £8 million which he spent in a similar fashion. Some of these were detailed by the Lloyd's committee of enquiry.

1) Interest-free loans made and repaid by using funds derived from the syndicates under the schemes: £1,817,000
2) The purchase, renovation, redecoration and maintenance of the villa La Doma acquired from Gregory Peck in the south of France: £5,890,000
3) Investment in the development of land in Florida: £480,597
4) Cash withdrawals in Geneva and London: £1,592,554
5) Investment in a diamond syndicate: £123,457
6) Investment in La Sierra, a Spanish company, whose business was that of selling orange juice: £244,242
7) Investments in films and musical productions: £1,692,081

8)   Expenses relating to Mr Dixon's boat: £270,387
9)   Expenses relating to an aircraft controlled by Mr Dixon: £122,206

James Adrian William Lunes Hardman, who had been a member since 1958, was more modest. Apart from receiving more than £70,000 in cash, discreetly in envelopes, he collected £21,000 in French and Swiss francs to pay for skiing holidays, and had his daughter's French school fees paid. All these interesting details were brought to light by Lloyd's own investigation, and so far it is only within Lloyd's that any disciplinary action has been taken. Cameron-Webb has made what has charmingly been designated as a 'timeous' resignation and removed himself first to the US and then to the refuge of one of his yachts in the Caribbean; Mr Dixon has been expelled and fined £1 million, which may or may not be collected, and has been traced to Virginia, where he lives in some luxury.

The present circumstances of Mr Dixon and Mr Cameron-Webb have provoked bitter comments, and invite comparisons with the fate of shop-lifters who may spend months in jail for taking something worth less than a hundred pounds.

But properly understood it is much to the credit of Lloyd's as an institution that it has pursued its own malefactors with such vigour and has not hesitated to do so. The deterrent effect of the publicity, quite apart from whatever possibility of punishment there may be, is considerable. It may seem rash, but I would suggest that it is unlikely that Lloyd's will see anything new of this sort again for some considerable time – which is not to say that the age-old practice of doubtful claims and the like will not continue, or that some other past offences may not even now be in the process of quiet interment.

Such gross malpractices at least enabled the new disciplinary measures to be tested, and it must be acknowledged that they have stood up creditably. Since 1982 the council has produced more than forty by-laws and regulations, stopping up a lot of holes; which might mean little had it not been for the energy with which they have been implemented. Eighteen cases, encompassing nearly thirty defendants, have been examined by the disciplinary committees. Penalties, varying from expulsions and fines of £1 million plus costs to reprimands, have been awarded.

The evidence collected by the Disciplinary Committee of Lloyd's, at the corporation's expense, was immediately passed to the Director of Public Prosecutions. This substantial amount of material included, in the PCW case, three volumes of the committee of enquiry report, with eighteen supporting files of documents, all transcripts of the committee's hearings, and two accountants' reports.

All this was sent to the DPP between March and May 1984: two years later no action by him has been forthcoming, a lack of progress which indicates pretty clearly where the system is breaking down. The imagination boggles at the time that might be consumed if Lloyd's had not been willing to do much of the preparatory work.

Nor have internal remedies been lacking. Alexander Howden, under its new ownership, instituted a full investigation of the misdeeds now admitted by Mr Grob and his colleagues, collected what restitution was available, and made an offer of £16 million to members of the syndicates. This was accepted.

All these transactions were carried out in the full light of publicity; documents were despatched to all concerned, and are made available to any other member who wishes to see them. Once more, the contrast with the secretive procedures of the law is striking.

As a result of the reforms Lloyd's is a changed institution. The presence of external members on the council representing all external names is a safeguard against any future well-meaning attempt to hush things up. Managing agents now make available copies of their accounts – much improved in reporting detail – which anyone may see. If there were to be a Freedom of Information Act in the UK, a thought that sends shivers of horror through the Civil Service, Lloyd's would not have to alter any of its procedures.

'Ten years ago', Peter Miller commented, 'a members' agent asking underwriters for information would be sent off with a flea in his ear: today the information would be willingly given.' Self-interest alone demands it, and self-interest, once understood, is a more powerful spur to action than any amount of external regulation.

Grumbling about Lloyd's has not yet subsided. As well as the Berrill recommendations on administration, a committee of enquiry on regulatory arrangements under Sir Patrick Neill was established 'to consider whether the regulatory arrangements which are being established at Lloyd's ... provide protection for the interests of members ... comparable to that proposed for investors under the Financial Services Bill'.

In its invitation to provide evidence the committee succinctly set out what it saw as the opposing views on Lloyd's:

a) On the one hand it is said that the Lloyd's Act 1982 has only been in operation for some three years; that in that time great energy has been devoted by Lloyd's in bringing to book those responsible for past malpractices; that many new by-laws and regulations and two codes of practice have been published; and that it would be a mistake for Parliament to intervene in any way (whether by the imposition of a new regulatory structure or otherwise) and thereby to interrupt the good work already in hand.

b)   On the other hand the critics urge that not enough has been done to put matters right; that some persons alleged to be guilty of past malpractices have not been pursued with sufficient zeal; and that the importance of Lloyd's business is such, and the links between its reputation and that of the rest of the City is so close, that Lloyd's cannot be allowed to continue without some form of external supervision.

It can hardly be argued that Lloyd's has not pursued malefactors to the limits of its ability. Indeed, it is well recognized that to do so is essential both to the good name of Lloyd's (which is more a pious phrase; insurance is an industry where reputation is all-important) and to satisfy the anger of names who have incurred losses and who can be relied upon not to take it lying down but to defend their own interests stoutly. (But I would not be sure that if a scandal might be thereby avoided potentially embarrassing matters might still not, in the old way, be quietly let drop.)

To insist: Lloyd's is a market. In the Middle Ages, when markets were the lifeblood of trade, and their orderly conduct imperative, justice was administered not by the ordinary courts, but as every schoolboy recalls, Piepowder courts, wherein disputes were settled by the specialists themselves, on the spot.

The disciplinary committee of Lloyd's is their modern equivalent and can be left alone to do the job. The alternative of regulation by the Department of Trade has been incontrovertibly proved inadequate.

PART FIVE

Always keep a hold of Nurse

12

Regulation

'And always keep a hold of Nurse
For fear of finding something worse.'

HILAIRE BELLOC

All regulation is very much a matter of locking stable doors after the horse has gone, but the situation in the City of London at present more closely resembles the construction of doors being carried out by a number of committees even before the stables have been erected and without any clear idea of the number, size and degree of wilfulness of the animals therein to be confined.

Lloyd's look upon themselves as having done their bit, and are annoyed at suggestions still being made that they should be in some way brought under the control of another body, and particularly resented the almost hysterical language of Leon Brittan, one of the mayfly secretaries of Trade and Industry, in the *Sunday Times* on 22 November 1985:

> If the authorities at Lloyd's do not show a diligent and responsible exercise of the significant powers they already have – and by this I mean DEMONSTRATING rigorous and effective enforcement, MAINTAINING the highest standards of conduct and having rule to STAMP OUT MALPRACTICE – then I would have no hesitation in introducing legislative action by the government.

For the rest, it looks at the moment to be something like the organization (if that is not an entirely inappropriate word) chart shown here. While one can be confident that whatever system eventually evolves will not be the same, since intentions change weekly, it must be admitted that the picture shown is not remarkable for its clarity.

At least the Bank of England's position remains straightforward enough: the prescription repeated in a stronger dose. When the White Paper on Banking Supervision appeared in December 1985 it became clear that, once again, the Bank of England's views had prevailed.

Table 9: Regulatory authorities

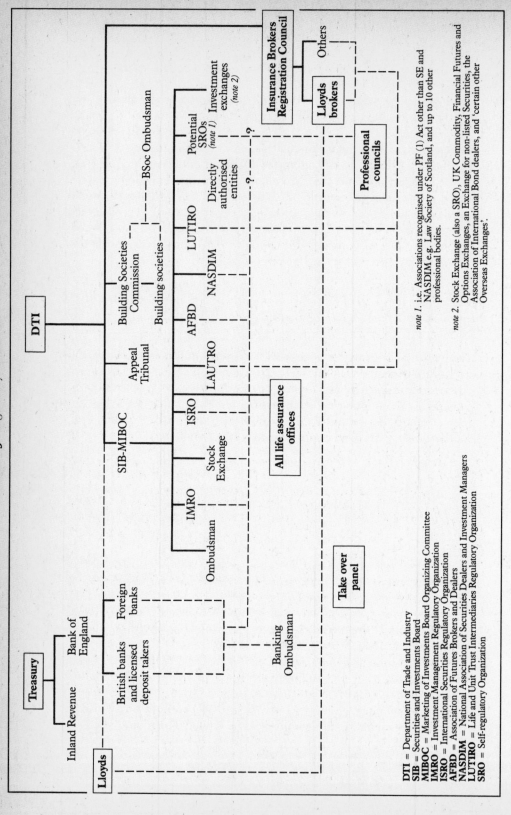

DTI = Department of Trade and Industry
SIB = Securities and Investments Board
MIBOC = Marketing of Investments Board Organizing Committee
IMRO = Investment Management Regulatory Organization
ISRO = International Securities Regulatory Organization
AFBD = Association of Futures Brokers and Dealers
NASDIM = National Association of Securities Dealers and Investment Managers
LUTIRO = Life and Unit Trust Intermediaries Regulatory Organization
SRO = Self-regulatory Organization

note 1. i.e. Associations recognised under PF (1) Act other than SE and NASDIM e.g. Law Society of Scotland, and up to 10 other professional bodies.

note 2. Stock Exchange (also a SRO), UK Commodity, Financial Futures and Options Exchanges, an Exchange for non-listed Securities, the Association of International Bond dealers, and 'certain other Overseas Exchanges'.

The circumstances which led to the rescue by the Bank of England of Johnson Matthey Bankers in October 1984 thus raised issues going far wider than the affairs of JMB itself. Accordingly, in December 1984 I [the Chancellor of the Exchequer] set up a Committee under the Chairmanship of the Governor of the Bank of England to look into our system of banking supervision and make recommendations.

The Leigh-Pemberton Committee's Report, published in June 1985, made it clear that while the JMB débâcle represented a wholly atypical lapse in a system of supervision that has had a good record over the years, and which compares well with the experience of financial centres overseas, there nevertheless remained serious weaknesses both in the implementation of banking supervision in the United Kingdon and in its statutory framework, the Banking Act of 1979.

The first proposal was for a new Board of Banking Supervision to be provided by statute. At first sight this might seem to be a strengthening of control against the Bank of England's wishes; after all, in 1975, the then Governor had argued against such actions:

Many would hold that a statute was necessary to remove any doubt in the minds of the public, and most especially of the banking community, about the standing of the supervisory authority and the nature of the process ... (but there are) some powerful arguments on the other side. For example, it is by no means clear to me that a non-statutory body will in practice be more cautious than a statutory one ...

But the statutory Board of Banking Supervision was to have only the most limited degree of independence.

The Government have considered whether the supervisory authority should be separate from the Central Bank. In principle, there are advantages in a separate banking supervisory organization. There may sometimes be conflicts of interest between the objectives of banking supervision and other Central Bank functions. It is clearly open to argument whether such tensions are best resolved within one institution. A separate organization would also lend itself to the establishment of a permanent core of expertise and professionalism in supervision. It would provide a clear focus for discussion and debate on supervisory issues. It could be made directly accountable to Parliament.

The Government have nevertheless decided to reject radical change in the organization of banking supervision in the United Kingdom. They do not consider that any advantages from such major institutional change could outweigh the inevitable loss of continuity and administrative upheaval. In the context of the United Kingdom's financial markets and institutions, the Government believe that the aims of supervision will best be met by continuing the established role of the Bank of England as supervisory authority but with the introduction of certain major organization changes.

The new Board was to function 'within the Bank', and was to be set up as soon as possible on a non-statutory basis until the new legislation took effect. Radical change was most certainly rejected, and progress was to be made in the blandest fashion. The Board was to be established by – the Governor of the Bank of England. Its members were to be appointed by – the Governor of the Bank of England (with the agreement of the Chancellor of the Exchequer). They were to be paid by – the Bank of England. Their task – 'to assist the Governor in the performance of his banking supervisory duties'. Their powers – 'If on any occasion he [the Governor] disagreed with the view of the Board's outside members, the Governor would still have the power to disregard their advice. But if he was to do so, he would have to inform the Chancellor of the Exchequer.'

It is no secret that the Treasury has been anxious to extend its control over the Bank of England, and through the Bank to the City; and in pursuance of that ambition it was supposed that Mr Robin Leigh-Pemberton would not exhibit the same degree of independence that his predecessor, Lord Richardson, had vigorously shown. The White Paper seems to indicate that the Treasury has not been successful. The Old Lady's power remains intact, the Board of Banking Supervision in its emasculated form looking like the merest gesture towards any limitation on the historic freedom of movement of the Governor.

A new Board of Banking Supervision also calls into question the role of the Court of Directors, as the board of the Bank of England is known. Never having much more than the appearance of power, which is concentrated in the hands of the executive directors and the Committee of Treasury, the most important of the Court committees, either the Court or the Board of Banking Supervision must surely become virtually meaningless.

None of this matters too much while professional bankers like George Blunden are at the head of affairs. But the lack of any effective board to monitor the executive director raises the question: *Quis custodiet ipsos custodes?* Especially if a government shows a record in other spheres of unremittingly political appointments (that of the present Governor is seen as a political appointment by the Opposition, but not universally by the City: neither of these opinions however are anything other than predictable in the circumstances).

The answer to Juvenal's question is probably that we will continue to rely upon the guardians to monitor their own activities. Any circumscription on the Bank's freedom to act with proper despatch gravely imperils crisis management ability, and nothing does so more than government interference. The White Paper suggests no such intention: indeed, with the Bank's supervisory mechanism overhauled and enlarged, it can be expected to take a more positive role in controlling banking institutions.

After the 1973 secondary banking crisis George Blunden had pointed out that the necessity for regulations had to be clear if Bank control was to be effective or even possible. 'It has never been possible for the Bank to impose supervision on organizations arbitrarily to meet our own wishes. There has always been the need for an obvious cause acceptable to the supervised to justify any extension of our supervision.'

The Johnson Matthey affair, and the international loan defaults, certainly provide an 'obvious cause' and the White Paper's proposals reflected the experience of these unsettling events. One proposal indicating this intention stands out as a milestone in that it is the first time that the Bank has set rules for the prudential regulation of lending. Hitherto the Bank has maintained that it was up to the boards of banks to manage their own business; how much they lent, and to whom, was their own affair, as long as they obeyed whatever guidelines were then in force. Controls had been confined to capital/risk ratios, which were advisory rather than mandatory, but in the White Paper and in discussion documents the Bank now makes it clear that it intends to place qualitative restrictions on the size of individual loans.

Banks must not only report all advances to a single borrower or related borrowers that exceed 10 per cent of the lending bank's capital and reserves (10 per cent has always been regarded as a prudent limit, the breach of which necessitates some degree of explanation), but an absolute ban is placed on all loans in excess of 25 per cent of the bank's own assets.

Had such a regulation been in force, the Johnson Matthey exposure to Nigeria would certainly have been spotted (always presuming that proper returns were made to the Bank of England) and in all probability some of the clearers' loans to Latin America would never have been made. It is a measure of banks' present nervousness that no objections have been raised to this radical diminution of their prerogatives.

The Bank of England also proposes to enlist the services of banks' auditors to report possible breaches of regulation or worse. The Johnson Matthey affair focused attention on the role of the banks' auditors, the question being what business had the auditors to certify in the 1984 accounts that the accounts 'give a true and fair view of the state of affairs of the company ... and of the result and source and application of funds of the group and comply with the Companies Act 1948–81', when the bank had at that time already committed actions which had lost half of its capital.

There are however many defences for this seemingly serious omission. The auditors of a firm manufacturing motor cars would not be expected to certify that the cars produced were in every way satisfactory and of high quality. Their task is to ensure that the books of the business are properly kept and the accounts reflect the financial position: unless there were to be an upsurge of warranty claims or actions for negligence the quality of the cars would not concern them. Indeed it is quite obvious that this is a subject on which a firm of accountants would find it impossible to comment.

As the business of a motor manufacturer is to make cars, so the business of a bank is to take deposits and make loans (leaving aside for the moment the other financial services offered by many, but not all, banks). Just because loans, unlike motor cars, are written in figures on bits of paper, is an auditor any more qualified to pronounce on their quality? He is no more a banker than he is an engineer.

Furthermore, in a manufacturing company a careful check of physical stock and work in progress against records should establish precisely the value of that part of the assets (although one would do well to remember how such confidence tricksters as Tino de Angelis were able to deceive the largest and most experienced financial institutions headed by American Express, into believing that millions of gallons of water were in fact the finest of salad oils) but, should bank staff be party to the deception, it requires no skill at all to conceal a fraudulent bank loan, for some considerable time, merely by juggling bits of paper and figures in a computer.

For such understandable reasons the accountancy profession is reluctant to accept further responsibilities, but the Bank of England and the Government are insisting that bank auditors assume a new duty of communicating any suspicions of irregularities to the Bank of England, if necessary behind their client's back. Should the profession not agree voluntarily, legislation will be passed to make the proposals compulsory:

> The Government accept that in the great majority of cases it will be desirable for both auditors and their clients to participate in the dialogue with supervisors; for discussions to be held on a trilateral basis, correspondence between the auditor and supervisor to be channelled through the authorised institution. However, the Government consider it necessary also to provide in exceptional cases for direct contacts between auditors and supervisors, without the knowledge of the supervised institution. There would be those few cases, for example involving suspected fraud, where it could be expected that the interests of deposi-

tors would be damaged if the bank's management were to know of the contact.

The above proposals involve new obligations for authorised institutions, but if the dialogue between auditors and supervisors is to play its full part in the supervisory process, then new obligations will also fall on auditors. Under the new arrangements auditors must be prepared to participate fully and openly in the communications process involving their clients, the supervisors and themselves and that will entail the delivery of independently held professional views as well as reporting on the accuracy and relevance of information about their clients' affairs. The Government attach great importance to these proposals and would be prepared if necessary to introduce legislation to establish auditors' obligations to supervisors. However, discussions are currently under way between the Bank of England and bodies representing the banks and the auditing profession, to seek to agree guidelines on the lines set out in Annex 4, which would avoid the need for such legislation.

While the effort being made to establish a second line of control through banks' auditors is explicitly with the example of Johnson Matthey in mind, another Leigh-Pemberton committee initiative seems also to be a consequence of the sort of problem Midland let themselves in for when buying Crocker. That is the suggestion that banks should involve their non-executive directors more closely in the affairs of bank lending.

4.1 The management of a bank lies in the hands of its directors and executives. It is not the function of either the auditors or the supervisors to take over the role of management; they all have their own discrete functions.

4.2 In our view, it is most important that all the directors, not only those in executive positions, involve themselves in a bank's affairs. In particular, non-executive directors should ensure that they are given sufficient information to be able to satisfy themselves that the policy guidelines and systems approved by the Board are being followed. We also believe that this is essential in order that the non-executive directors are able to make a constructive contribution to the direction of the bank's business, including forming their own view of the quality of its lending and other risk assets.

4.3 Audit committees, which are normally composed largely of non-executive directors, can play a particularly useful role in monitoring the operations of a bank. To do so, however, they must not restrict their activities to matters related to the preparation of the annual accounts. They must become involved in assessing and monitoring the bank's control systems and receiving reports from both internal and external auditors.

4.4 Banks have been relatively slow to follow the example of commercial companies and appoint finance directors to their boards. This may be understandable in the sense that all the executive directors are 'financial'. We believe however that there is an important role to be played by a finance director who, apart from the managing director and the chairman, will be best placed to take an overall view of the business. It is not an easy role, as the finance director must be prepared to question and challenge the decisions of his colleagues, but it can be a most important one. JMB had neither a finance director nor an audit committee ...

4.6 If the auditors and the supervisor are to be able to assist each other to carry out their respective functions there must be a dialogue between them. The process is at present hindered by the confidentiality constraints on both parties. The auditors of a bank have the same duties under the Companies Acts as the auditors of other companies. The auditors are appointed by the shareholders and report to them. Under present conventions and practices auditors feel constrained by the duty of confidentiality which they owe to their client not to disclose information to third parties including the supervisors. The supervisors, for their part, are bound by the confidentiality provision in Section 19 of the Banking Act from disclosing information obtained in the course of supervision to the auditors.

If an audit committee is to be effective it would need a very different sort of board from that normally found in banks, where the conduct of business lies firmly with the full-time professionals while the part-time (often very part-time indeed) directors can do little more than nod assent.

The function of non-executive directors in banks deserves rather more discussion. The Midland Bank, for example, has more than 80,000 employees operating in twenty countries whose activities comprise merchant and investment banking, hire purchase and leasing, as well as domestic and international banking. It is unrealistic to expect part-time, non-executive directors to see more than a fraction of what goes on.

Nor, often enough, are directors equipped to understand the growing complexities of financial issues. Being sensible men and women they are conscious of this and do not seek to meddle with the nuts and bolts. Their acquiescence is taken for granted. Banking directors have a particularly difficult task; it is almost impossible for them, as for the auditors, to get at the facts of what is happening at a bank. The director of a manufacturing company can visit the factories and showrooms and, if he knows anything about industry at all, pick up the signals that will enable him to interpret and flesh out the board reports he receives. This cannot be done with the branch of a bank, where nothing other than the most subjective judgement is possible. A bank director remains entirely dependent upon the information with which he is fed.

A non-executive director of a bank is not usually expected to take more than the most general interest in the operations of his company, and he is remunerated accordingly. Seven out of the eight non-executives on the board of the Midland, for example, were paid less than £10,000 in 1985, an indication of the restricted nature of their obligations.

The normal practice of any bank is to conduct business by a series of delegations: the board will allow the chief executive, alone or in concert with others, discretion to advance up to a given sum. This might be, for example, not to exceed 10 per cent of a bank's capital. Overall limits of lending to countries are established: certain areas may be interdicted: (loans for armaments or to South Africa, for example, were banned in Grindlays); special limits may be placed on others such as property or shipping.

The chief executive in turn will delegate his powers to divisional directors, and they to management. Large, or controversial, loans have to work their way up the system. If such a loan does so, not falling by the wayside, it is possible that it might have to go to the board itself for approval. But since boards meet only at intervals, and business must go on in a prompt and timely fashion, such scrutiny would be unusual. More generally, a committee of the board will examine major loans only after they have been made on the authority of management.

In either instance it is difficult to the point of near impossibility for a board composed mainly of non-executive directors, many of whom have no experience of banking, to gainsay the considered opinion of those who have. They will let things pass.

This characteristic is not confined to banks. In an interesting Harvard study made by Professor Myles Mace, *Directors – Myth and Reality*, he concluded that 'The board's statutory duty to manage the business is a myth.' It might be that they were able to define corporate stategy and broad policies but the objectives were established by executives. Nor did directors, in any but a formal sense, elect their chairman, who was usually nominated by the retiring chairman, assisted perhaps by a cabal: new directors were appointed in the same way and once in place it was regarded as 'discourteous', or a 'breach of corporate management' to challenge executives or even to ask discerning questions, or in any way to 'rock the boat'. Harold Williams, chairman of the SEC, observed that 'dissenting directors, are, however, rare and for some reason, they often seem to have short tenure ... the board ... insulates management rather than holding it accountable'.

Johnson Matthey Bankers is by no means the only bank to have neither a finance director or an audit committee, and the decision-making processes of bank boards continue to be shaky. Non-executive directors usually (but not invariably: one well-known clearing bank director was notorious for catching up on his sleep during board meetings) comprise men, and even occasionally women, of clear distinction and experience. Having doubtless studied the voluminous papers sent to them with due care and attention, they turn up for meetings at best once a month and face an agenda of which many have only the remotest of comprehension. In the days when a clearing bank's business was concerned with funding UK-based companies and citizens, the system worked well enough, but with the increasing complexity of banking the dangers of directors having the most tenuous grasp of what is going on and spending only a very short time on their bank's business is apparent. It is difficult to believe that the Midland's affair with Crocker could have developed as it did otherwise.

Executives do not much relish the task of explaining (if indeed they understand themselves; the development of new techniques has been so rapid that those now at the head of affairs have often no direct experience of what it is their subordinates are doing) the agenda to their part-time colleagues, and as a result boards are often not brought into discussion of even major policy decisions. Instead a more-or-less closely argued *fait accompli* is presented to them for their rubber stamp.

This has it dangers. When Grindlays were approached in 1983 by the ANZ Bank the board as a whole were not made aware of it until the matter was finalized. They did not much object to this, since the offer was so clearly advantageous to Grindlays' shareholders as to make discussion unnecessary. The subsequent general evacuation by very nearly the whole of Grindlays' management as ANZ began their delayed integration could well have been avoided, however, had there been more open discussion. It is hard to believe that boards are not similarly treated when the result is not so favourable to shareholders.

The lessons of such experiences have been understood by the Bank of England and are the reason why such stress is laid on the responsibilities of finance directors, audit committees and auditors: banks, conscious of their own deficiencies are not inclinded to argue.

Montagu Norman's tradition of shoulder-patting or arm-twisting, over cups of tea, with secrecy surrounding every move, has been replaced by a more open approach, which was developing even before the reassessments of the 1980s. The Radcliffe committee had something to do with this, when in its report of 1959 it included the observation that 'a special responsibility rests on the central bank for the gathering and publication of such [financial statistical] information', and invited the Bank of England 'to give consideration to ... the issue of a quarterly bulletin in which could appear either some of the more technical discussions of monetary issues and signed articles on more controversial matters', and to 'take a lead in promoting and inspiring the objective study of monetary and financial problems'. The idea was not accepted with universal enthusiasm. While the clearers were prepared – as be they must – to give information to the Bank they were anxious, especially when times were bad, that this remain confidential. The Radcliffe committee also recognized that the Bank itself might feel constrained 'because they would not feel free to say more than was consistent with ministerial utterances'.

Neither objection prevailed, and with increasing enthusiasm and skill the Bank has since produced more than 100 issues of its quarterly bulletin. Not only does this give the most valuable information as to what takes place in the financial world, but offers an opportunity for Bank directors to fly, in the most discreet manner possible, some interesting kites, sometimes by no means consistent with ministerial utterances.

In a recent issue David Walker, an executive director who joined the Bank from the Treasury, an unusual step, examined the difficulties facing companies which had to concentrate, especially in a period of recession, on short-term targets, blurring their ability to plan strategically on the much longer term that the cost and complexity of modern industry demands.

> But beyond these reasons for board concern with the short term there is the fact that, disagreeable as the need to focus exclusively on survival may be, it tends to involve much less intellectual and imaginative business endeavour than choosing a long-term strategy. Planning for long-term survival in an environment that is cash-rich may be much more difficult than striving to survive in a situation of severe short-term pressures. This problem is now reinforced for British boards by a complex of factors that are perhaps best summed up as their perceptions and apprehensions about the behaviour of others, including their shareholders. Over and above the fact that horizons of institutions have shortened, we have the phenomenon that boards may often believe them to have done so to an exaggerated extent and thus adapt their own behaviour and decision-making accordingly, with large efforts made to avoid short-term earnings dips.

> These concerns are sharpened by the much greater apprehension at the risk of takeovers which, given the rapid acceleration in acquisition and merger activity, is hardly surprising.

... these factors may be exerting significant effects on corporate behaviour. They underscore an attitude that attention to the longer run is a luxury and risk that can be indulged only within tight limits, specially by companies that see themselves as potential takeover targets.

Mr Walker was by no means the first to air these problems, which were clear enough in the 1970s, when the Labour Party devoted a number of working parties and study groups to the subject of attracting investment to industry. In the latest of these, published in 1982, 'The City, A Socialist Approach', the creation of a National Investment Bank, which would 'provide long-term lending to companies as part of packages of financial support designed to encourage investment in a framework of industrial planning' was suggested. The NIB would be funded in part by instructing institutions to repatriate a proportion of their overseas investments and to deploy at least some of these into approved domestic investment. This concept is still in the front of Labour Party policy, but hardly justifies the epithet of socialist, since it does no more than reflect French practice since 1945 and much of US policy in the 1960s and 1970s.

Mr Walker treads a cautious path around the proposal to form an NIB, justly remarking that 'ultimately, the question whether we have such an institution is a political one', but goes on to examine an alternative in which

institutions should set aside or hypothecate part of their UK equity portfolio in respect of which they should deliberately take a longer-term view. To some extent, this goes with the grain of what some large – and some not so large – institutions have already chosen to do, for example in committing a specified percentage of their portfolios to non-listed stakes in 'high-tech', or small ventures, to establish and secure accept-ance that part of the UK equity portfolio of an institution need not be so actively turned over in the market, and the more institutions accepted this, the easier it would be for any one manager deliberately to choose to hold particular stakes on a term basis. An individual fund manager cannot readily withdraw on his own from the short-term performance business but might feel able to do so in respect of part of his portfolio if he were confident that others were proceeding similarly.

Cast in other terms, such an approach would acknowledge a fund manager should have more than one objective. The concentration of savings has concentrated large influence in some investor hands and the managers concerned are properly interested in maximising some combination of capital gain and income in a particular time period. But, if the time scale is so uniformly short that other priorities suffer, the risk of policy interference to limit institutional freedom of manoeuvre is bound to increase. In this situation, it seems worth considering whether institutional investors might not disclose perhaps on an annual basis, the turnover of different parts of their equity portfolio and some indication of the broad areas by which they expected to be relatively committed holders in the period ahead, and of the portfolio percentage involved in them. This would not of course involve commitment to holdings in any particular company, but by reducing the proportion of equity portfolios in respect of which short-term performance is expected it would help to redress the imbalance in the present situation.

This sort of cool and intelligent approach contrasts so clearly with the one-sided partisanship usual at Westminster as to emphasize the necessity for ensuring the Bank of England's continued independence from Treasury intervention. Armed with powerful new authority, if not much assisted by the Board of Banking Supervision, the Bank of England is well placed to monitor the traditional banking business, although how far this can be extended to the new Euromarkets remains to be seen.

13

The Old Lady's new problems

'Resolved that some of the Bank of England be spoke
to and that it be seen what assistance they can give.'

THE LORDS JUSTICES, 1696

Having neatly assembled all banks, proper and improper, fully fledged
and the merest nestlings, under the Old Lady's wise jurisdiction, a cuckoo
shows every sign of taking up residence. Just as the 123-banks reported to
the Board of Trade, escaping the surveillance of the Bank of England, so,
ultimately, do the building societies.

Some building societies are large (but so were some 123-banks) and all
are very respectable (but the Bank of England must have considered all
160 licensed deposit-takers respectable). Some have only a handful of
shareholders and a million or so of capital. Yet building societies are
rapidly assuming, more than ever did 123-banks, all the functions of a
bank 'proper', while remaining outside the control of the Bank of England.
Their activities are instead overseen by the Chief Registrar of Friendly
Societies, who doubles as the Industrial Assurance Commissioner, and is
a Civil Servant over whose decisions the Bank of England has no influence.

At present this can lead to little unease, for building societies have been
on the whole very well behaved, apart from the odd picturesque scandal,
which has been solved by having a larger society absorb the offending
brother. Self-regulation is practised by the Building Societies' Association
which acts as an effective monitor and to help in times of trouble.

The movement reflects, with an astonishing accuracy, British middle-
class values. It is the average Englishman's (Scots are more partial to
rented accommodation) ambition to own his own, freehold, home. A
survey made in 1985 revealed the height of human felicity, as seen by that
mythical figure, to be sitting by his own fireside, watching a video, and
eating a take-away meal. The most essential component of this not altogether disagreeable vision is the home, and the building society the most
popular and available means of acquiring it.

Home ownership is very big business: over 70 per cent of heads of households are home owners, and borrow a total of £126 billion (at the end of 1985). Of this, 77 per cent, some £96 billion, comes from the building societies, and finances an even greater proportion of purchases. Insurance-based loans, which tend to be larger, or bank loans, are used for more expensive properties: it is the building society that is the mainstay of popular home ownership.

Advances have been made possible by deposits from the same segment of society that are, at different times, borrowers. Between 1957 and 1983 the societies' share of savings grew from 5.5 to 16.4 per cent; over 25 million people now have building society accounts, and a high proportion of these are substantial – over 60 per cent of the total is represented by 5 million accounts of over £5,000, while in 1983/4 half a million new depositors invested more than £10,000 each.

These peculiarly Anglo-Saxon institutions have flourished for a couple of centuries, and been exported throughout the English-speaking world. They originate in that working-class tradition of self-help that gave birth to friendly societies, mutual insurance companies, savings banks and the Co-operative movement (it is often forgotten that even today a very substantial proportion of the economy is attributable to these non-capitalist institutions). The earliest societies were local, even parochial, consisting of a few members whose savings were used to finance house purchase, the recipient often being chosen by lot. This local knowledge, both of the value of the property and the reliability of the borrower, was an essential reason for the success of the societies. In much the same way American banks, far too small to be safe or effective by European standards, but being very alive to local personalities and events, continue to give support to their communities in a way that the Big Four cannot match. It is an interesting speculation that much of the flexibility of the US economy may be due to small enterprises being able to borrow from bankers possessing personal knowledge of both businesses and borrowers.

Although now grown far beyond their modest origins the character of building societies has not essentially changed. Every depositor, however small, is still a member, entitled to vote at AGMs and to propose motions for consideration, a right which is determinedly exercised.

Even so large and sophisticated an institution as Nationwide, the third largest building society, with assets of £10,000 million, and the first to issue stock-exchange-quoted bonds, reflects its democratic roots. All members were circulated in 1985, as in every other year, with the report and accounts, together with the agenda of the AGM. This contained the proposals by way of special resolutions for consideration at the meeting that members had been pleased to advance. One member, Ms S. Elder, put forward the entertaining suggestions that 'the National Anthem shall be played at the conclusion of each General Meeting of members commencing with immediate effect', and that 'an Honorary Chaplain to the Society shall be appointed to lead members in prayer at the commencement of each General Meeting'. With such great matters do the three-and-a-half million members have to concern themselves! It is probable that not too many members trouble themselves; of the ten proposals listed, three came from a Mrs Davis, one from a Mr Davis, one from a Mr Yeomans and three from Mr C. F. J. Punt, a solicitor: Mr Punt was also nominated for election to the board.

The boards of societies are those which might be expected to suit the membership, composed of non-executive members of the highest reputation, together with the senior officers of the society, very much after the style of a clearing bank. The non-executives do quite well, seven at Nationwide being paid over £10,000, which is more than they would be likely to get on the board of a much larger bank for what ought to be more onerous duties. A tell-tale sign to the *cognoscenti* is that several directors list a fellowship of the Royal Society of Arts after their name, a practice that would raise eyebrows in more sophisticated circles.

All in fact is redolent of the decent, honest, God-fearing lower middle classes; Morris cars, Tyrolean hats, short motoring coats, low churchmanship, caravans and six o'clock supper – the backbone, in truth, of the country. Lest these observations appear cynically superior I should emphasize that they are offered affectionately rather than in any critical spirit, in an attempt to indicate graphically the strengths and weaknesses of the movement.

These strengths have tempted the societies to disregard the warning issued in 1969 by the Governor of the Bank of England on the perils of muscling in on high-street banking business. 'I suggest that Building Societies should resist any temptation that they may feel – and which Saturday closing of banks might sharpen – to try to launch out further into the banking field.'

The warning can hardly have proved effective, for six years later not only did building societies offer immediate withdrawal facilities, on a 24-hour basis, long opening hours, cash machines, credit cards, travellers' cheques and free standing orders, but they had begun to muscle in on the lending prerogatives of the banks, in that they were offering to make loans, based on the traditional security of property, but available for a wide range of purposes and with a considerable degree of informality.

The bigger societies are looking to extend their freedom of movement: and the Building Societies Bill, put before Parliament early in 1986, will if passed enable a building society to do everything that a high-street bank could do for the personal customer.

For what has been a traditional and conservative industry has begun in recent years to move very fast indeed. In addition to allowing unsecured lending the Building Societies Bill also provides that the societies may, with the assent of 20 per cent of the members, change their status to a public limited company, a move likely to precipitate a rush of takeovers and radically alter the nature of the movement. The Nationwide at least is being cautious about this, having regard to the special relationship it sees as existing between the society and its customers, but will probably extend into those other financial services which the Act will make possible. These are many and varied: societies will be able to own and develop their own land, opening the way to a merger with housing associations, local enterprise agencies and others, not only in the existing friendly society movement, which remains a significant force in this area, but with commercial developers. Societies will be able to provide cheque books, cheque cards, and overdrafts or personal loans, in addition to the cash withdrawal facilities, travellers' cheques and currency, and credit cards already available. Like the Post Office they will be able to sell government securities and National Savings Certificates. They may give advice and arrange for the purchase and sale of securities, arrange insurance, provide surveys and valuations. They may manage and sell unit trusts and provide tax advice.

Developments in data transmission make it possible to perform most of these activities in branch offices; indeed such societies as the Leicester have pioneered, in conjunction with banks, the provision of direct entry into customers' accounts from their own homes. It is already possible to operate a building society or a bank account through a Prestel link, and although this has so far developed slowly it seems certain to become progressively more popular.

Limitations will continue to exist, at least temporarily, since 90 per cent of assets must remain available for first-mortgage lending. Nevertheless the Nationwide at least intends to press forward with chequing accounts and credit cards.

All this will make a building society look very much like a high-street bank, but a problem looms; who are they going to do it with, for the human resources of building societies are nowhere near sufficient for the new and more sophisticated role they envisage for themselves?

The strengths of societies, which have made possible this rapid expansion, all too visible in the rash of branch offices in every small town, threaten accompanying dangers. One is that the demand for resources which has been created now goes beyond the funds made available by building society depositors, tempting societies to borrow in the wholesale market, which is seductive but not without danger, at a time when management expenses, fuelled by expansion, are rising. Such borrowings formed 5.5 per cent of building society funds in 1985, and are permitted by the Bill to rise to 20 per cent.

Such a gearing departs from the original principles on which societies operated. Although it is a cardinal rule of banking that ruin is guaranteed by borrowing short and lending long, this is precisely what building societies have done for generations, and to the extreme. They take in deposits, often sight deposits, and always on short term, and lend for periods of up to thirty years, on that most illiquid of assets, a borrower's home. Yet they have flourished for a couple of centuries by flagrant disregard of what other lenders consider the most elementary prudence.

There have been good reasons; in the last fifty years house prices have shown steady rises, thereby continuously improving the cover given to the loans in case of failure and, more importantly, since people are very reluctant indeed to be deprived of their houses, they are willing to undergo considerable privations in order to keep up with their payments. This state of things might now be changing, and evidence exists to show that defaults, in a time of crushing unemployment, have increased, and societies have become less reluctant to evict.

Unsecured lending bolted on to an existing structure of offices and management, provided by wholesale money, can be extremely profitable for societies anxious to diversify in the face of such changing circumstances; but it is one thing to have the powers to raise new capital and quite another to be able to employ it safely. Building society managers now in post have relied for their success upon an intimate knowledge of local housing conditions which has allowed them to gauge with some precision the value of the security: some areas are good, others bad; here semis may be in demand, there terrace housing acceptable; Nos. 1–20 in a street may be passable, but squatters begin at No. 21; houses built by Marjorie Daw are sound, those of the See-saw group disintegrating. Some criticism has been levelled at these standards as perpetuating inner city ghettos and as restricting innovatory techniques, but it is easy to appreciate how convenient societies find them.

Such skills are best acquired by experience, and do not demand the more sophisticated credit assessment and security perfection that is expected from branch bank managers. Not to put too fine a point on it, the operations of a building society branch office demands little intellectual or educational background beyond the simplest, and have accordingly been performed by people of decency and probity, but with considerable limitations. The likelihood, for example, of good graduates being attracted by building societies is minimal. In fact, according to the Cambridge University Appointments Board, only now, and then only among the bolder, are societies beginning to consider the matter; this year, for the first time, two societies may recruit their first graduate trainees. In the pool of talent available to them the societies start at the gravest of disadvantages. It is true that clearing banks did not take management recruitment seriously until quite recently, preferring to rely upon school leavers till the 1970s, but now take graduates in considerable numbers – 140 a year in the National Westminster – and invest heavily in their training.

Bank management development programmes and personnel departments are geared to process talent in considerable numbers; building societies will have to develop these skills from scratch. Yet is is not easy to see how the responsibilities of the new-style building society branch manager are going to differ from those of a retail bank manager. It is true that he will not be handling executor and trustee business, nor tax counselling, but banks deal with these in separate departments. Nor will a building society manager have corporate clients, but will deal only with individuals, though even this distinction is disappearing. The affairs of large businesses are today handled by bank head offices or area offices, or by the merchant banks in which all the major clearers now have interests. Even small businesses are tending to become the responsibility of specialist managers, as it becomes more difficult for even the banks to find competent managers for all branches.

Building societies face a steeply uphill task in matching human resources to their future plans, especially in view of the competition that is being shown by the clearers in fighting for the traditional base of building societies' business, the average home loan.

Having made one unsuccessful foray into the mortgage market in 1978/9 the clearing banks are now determined to regain lost ground. Bank mortgage loans rose from £500 million in 1980 to £5,000 million two years later, declining somewhat after that, but recovering strongly in the second half of 1985. Lloyds are particularly active, recognizing 'major battles' being fought over home loans, and owning, unique among banks, a chain of estate agencies, a field in which they claim to be 'clear market leaders' with 235 offices and a turnover of £1,500 million.

NatWest talks of 'fierce competition' and provides more mortgages than any other clearer through its subsidiary NW Home Loans, which made advances of £850 million in 1985, bringing its total mortgage book to £3,400 million.

Competition from building societies has produced further indirect changes as banks perceive the necessity to recover lost customers. The daft and self-defeating move of closing on Saturdays is being reversed, although at a pedestrian rate; Lloyds have 182 branches open out of 2,623, NatWest

190 out of 3,200, although it should be added that both banks are attempting to make Saturday trading distinctive. NatWest rely on cash machines, of which they have the largest network in the world, and make staff available to discuss customers' financial requirements. Lloyds do much the same thing, and have some branches open until 3 p.m.

It is ironic that American banks, working in what is meant to be a violent and crime-ridden society, have operated these open banking methods, now being hailed by British clearers as exciting new departures, for many years, while customers here have been herded into comfortless corridors, often with stockmarket-like pens to enable them to shuffle forward in due order, to be faced by a harassed clerk barely visible and entirely inaudible, behind bulletproof glass, and metal screens that would be counted excessive in one of Her Majesty's prisons.

A typical American bank branch is a much more agreeable place to visit. A large proportion of the space will be given over to staff sitting at desks ready to talk to customers. Those who merely want to make deposits or withdrawals can do so in decent human intercourse over a counter to friendly clerks not protected by a version of the Berlin Wall, and insulated thereby from any customer contact.

One senior clearing banker reacted with stunned distaste when I suggested that his sort of business, retail banking, was, after all, a sort of shopkeeping, which he clearly thought of as an inferior activity. As long as this attitude is common among his colleagues the clearers will have an uphill task in training staff to meet standards of customer treatment that building societies, for example, do not find too difficult to achieve.

A useful test – which works with hospital receptionists as well – is to respond to the grunt of acknowledgement, so commonly the only sign of one's presence, with a bright greeting, which if it produces anything more than a baffled surliness can be construed as a sign that not all is lost. There are, of course, banks and banks, and needless to say those banks where I transact my own affairs, which include branches of the NatWest and Midland, are remarkable for their charm and efficiency. A good manager can work miracles with his staff, but needs to do so when the amenities offered to his customers more nearly resemble those of a low-class betting shop or that ultimate in degradation, a British Rail station, than a civilized place of business.

But the penny is dropping. NatWest have even appointed an AGM in charge of marketing, John Green, who asks, 'What does the customer want? Where does he want it? And how can we provide it?'

Even though banks and building societies may start as favourites there are other runners in the race for the home loan market. Insurance companies have offered equity- and pension-linked mortgage loans for some years, and are now hoping to extend this business, which has been concentrated towards the more expensive properties, to their existing life customers.

The Prudential Insurance Co., based on a solid working-class connection, reflected in its magnificent Waterhouse headquarters in Holborn Bar, intends to expand its range of services radically. They have already converted their battalions (some 12,000) of foot soldiers who call at households every week to collect life premiums – and sell, where possible, a little more – to offering mortgages; and like Lloyds, the Pru have moved into the estate agency business.

The Pru's loyal customer base is a valuable asset in extending the financial services market, for the UK is one of the most underbanked of advanced countries, and the great unbanked present a formidable opportunity.

Like so many other things in our caste-ridden society the possession of a bank account can be seen as a class marker. Bank customers are rarer in the Midlands and North than in the rest of the country, among unskilled manual workers and pensioners, local authority tenants and early school-leavers. There is a close connection between reluctance to use banks and the custom of making wage payments weekly in cash, a practice to which workers in the older industrial areas remain faithfully attached. A seminar of bankers gathered in Cambridge in 1981 was presented with the statistics and an interpretation:

> It is very clear from research that the world of weekly pay and physical cash is substantially different from the world of monthly pay and abstract paper. The monthly-paid have financial problems, problems about how to make the best use of their incomes – and would like, at least in theory, advice about how to solve them. The weekly-paid have money difficulties – that is, simply not having enough of it. They have a strong emotional attachment to cash, which is physical and controllable; you cannot over-spend cash and your £ notes are as good as the next man's.
>
> Not only have they not felt the need for a more convenient system for paying monthly bills, but they are also fairly unenthusiastic about moving to monthly pay and the monthly-paid life-style. Fifty-five per cent of the weekly-paid said they would be 'quite unhappy' or 'very unhappy' to do so; only 15 per cent said they would be 'very' or 'quite happy'. When asked what would be the advantages of being paid monthly, 55 per cent couldn't think of any.
>
> Banks represent the monthly-paid, middle-class educated, office-working system of the 'haves'. They do not immediately suggest a universal human motivator as building societies do (the young couple

and 'our home') or even insurance companies do ('security for your loved ones').

A common manifestation of this fear of banks was an evident sense of inferiority when confronted with bank staff, either in reality or in imagination. Bank staff were assumed to adopt an insulting superior manner when dealing with ordinary members of the public, and also to be dauntingly well educated and well dressed. Such experience as these people had had of bank staff had evidently not shaken this feeling of inadequacy. Some of the men particularly showed signs of resentment at this posture, especially as they believed they probably earned more money than bank staff themselves.

Hopes of extending the proportion of the population availing themselves of the services offered by financial institutions are shared by others. Stockbrokers now regret the decline of the private investor and are campaigning to revive him. They have been encouraged by the apparent success of the British Telecom issue which, attracting over 2 million shareholders, succeeded in nearly doubling the number of individuals owning quoted securities. It was however a strictly limited success. According to a survey made a year afterwards the great majority of the new shareholders were typical middle-class, middle-aged savers who might be prepared to have a flutter on one or two similar issues but who had no intention of developing an active portfolio.

The City men were well aware they were on to a good thing, and attempts to make multiple acceptances took place on a grand scale. Many of these were of serious dimensions; the chief executive of one well-known bank was said to have benefited considerably, although it was without his knowledge, and he ensured restitution: other examples have been swept under the carpet or bogged down in the notoriously difficult route to the DPP.

More than a couple of generous new issues will be needed to stimulate wider shareholding. There is a good deal of ground to make up since apparently only 6 per cent of the population at present hold shares directly (this percentage is disputed, like all statistics, but represents the judgement of the Stock Exchange); the equivalent percentage in the US is 19. The decline has been sharp for, as recently as 1963, 59 per cent of all British equities were held by individuals.

Many other people own unit trust shares and indirectly, through life assurance and pension funds, individuals have substantial entitlements. These are likely to continue, at least in the medium term: when the number of pensioners with substantial entitlements grows, as it is expected to do over the next quarter century, a transfer may take place as relatively rich pensioners use their lump sum payments to invest directly in the stock market. In the meantime any switched capital must come from building society and bank deposits, National Savings and other forms of liquid assets.

It requires an eye of faith to see this happening without some assistance. The tax advantages of life assurance, the convenience of bank and building society deposits, and the frank unsophistication of many, make it seem doubtful, especially given the onset of a bear market.

In order to encourage a wider spread of shareholding, attention has been focused on such devices as the *Loi Monory* in France, which gives tax relief on the purchases of shares by individuals up to a maximum of 7,000 fr. per year, and allows their sale tax free after five years. The American Individual Retirement Account (which is of course known as the IRA, causing some alarm to British visitors) allows similar tax concessions.

Both these schemes have produced the desired result, in France causing the proportion of individual share ownership to rocket from the British to the American level in a few years.

The 1986 Budget proposals for the British equivalent, the Personal Equity Plan, are still being mulled over, it being clear to no one at this stage quite how the proposals might work. The modest ceiling (£2,400 p.a.) on protected investments mean that direct access to brokers for new investors would be expensive. Investment on this scale is more suited to unit trust purchases, but since it appears that shares must be bought directly either an intermediary or a great deal of advice will be needed.

The well-marked route to increased sophistication is by way of National Savings, Premium Bonds and other government forms of saving that can be bought direct at post offices, the only financial institution that serves all levels of the population. Industrial life companies such as the Prudential obviate the need to visit any office at all. Building societies are next; a high percentage of the subscription to the Telecom issue came from building society accounts and, as we have seen, building societies are regarded as easier to deal with than banks. The clearers try to provide investment advice, but their ability to do this is patchy. Serious investors deal direct with their stockbrokers.

If direct investment in shares is to become widespread it will most probably be through the medium of building societies or banks, and the race is on to see which can develop the best service. An investor requires to be satisfied on a number of points. He must have the mechanics of the market explained – the commissions and taxes involved, the account system, and buying and selling prices. Complexities like hedging through the option system or speculating with traded options need to be discussed. If he is to go outside the UK market currency risks have to be analysed. Some of this may well be done initially by providing printed matter, but personal advice is usually likely to be essential, and the provision of this to prove more difficult to building societies than to banks.

The actual performances of transactions presents little problem, for improved data transmission systems enable immediate quotations to be given and documentation issued. In experimental share shops, such as that run by Quilter Hilton and Goodison in Debenhams in Oxford Street, printed analyses of some recommended equities are provided, staff are prepared to advise, instant bargains can be struck by a direct line to the floor of the Exchange, and contract notes handed over. Direct dealing of this sort is also a protection against fraud. Most Stock Exchange frauds have been made possible by clients who were distanced, or who distanced themselves, from the transactions being carried out on their behalf.

Though the prospect of every man his own capitalist may be entertaining as a political theory, it is less so in the cold light of economic day. Any competent adviser would steer the small investor away from direct investment of the sort meant to be encouraged by the PEP. The minimum which can be handled economically is £100,000 or so, and the possession of a sum of that sort available for portfolio investment should assume other substantial underlying assets kept in more liquid form, all a far cry from £200 a month.

One advantage that might be claimed for common capitalist man is that the habit of investment would encourage the growth of small businesses by enabling entrepreneurs to tap new funds. This is purely fallacious. Even if it were prudent to allow direct investment on a small scale it would be an act of irresponsibility to place this anywhere except in the bluest of chips. The over-the-counter market and business investment start-ups are most decidedly not for the small investor except as an alternative to football pools and the tote. Whether the average investor who fancies a flutter, and the breed is common in Britain, will be unduly deterred by thoughts of prudence, is open to question. An intriguing insight into behavioural psychology will be offered when it is seen whether building societies or banks get the business. Banks are seen to be (and rightly so) more knowledgeable, but building societies are now the accepted repository of savings.

High-street competition for the clearers will be sharpened by the expansion of the Trustee Savings Banks, which if taken together already form the biggest retail bank, with over 6 million customers. The TSB is preparing a public offering, which is expected to add £1,000 million to its capital.

Like the building societies, TSB lacks the depth of management possessed by the clearing banks: unlike the building societies it has realized this and initiated a comprehensive training and recruitment scheme. Three more banks – Standard Chartered, the Bank of Scotland and the Royal Bank of Scotland – have also joined the clearing system. The latter is adopting a strongly forward policy in retail banking, while the Bank of Scotland has pioneered 'home banking' which offers customers direct access to their accounts via Prestel, and is regarded as being very much the shape of things to come, although still in the stage of development which requires the keying of forty-seven digits before access is achieved.

Although information on specified accounts is now available through the cash dispensing system, bank computers are not yet generally geared to the scale of real-time operation that this sort of activity will require, as thousands of customers all want information at the same time on Saturday mornings. When this becomes possible the necessity for high-street premises will be reduced. Payments that are not made by direct debit can be electronically transferred; smaller sums of cash can be obtained from card machines. Cards are being currently used in experiments by both Midland and NatWest for direct debiting at point of sale, which if successful (and one of the snags is that the magnetic strip on the card which conveys the information is easily damaged by contact with other cards) may complete the transition to chequeless banking, for it is that, rather than cashless banking, that is in sight.

Yet more competition is threatened by the Post Office Girobank, which already has 2 million customers and 5 per cent of the personal banking market. Recognizing the impossibility of loading the already strained post office network with more customers, Girobank intends to offer a full range of banking services using postal and telephone services linked with cash dispensing machines. Every customer will be given a named account executive who will (theoretically) be available on the telephone (if you can get through).

This sounds unenticing. Much of the appeal of banks is the speedy access they provide to qualified staff, of whom there are precious few in Girobank. It is more likely that Girobank may act as another link in the chain that already exists between post offices, building societies, and banks.

Specialist institutions are also springing up – the Mortgage Corporation, owned by Salomon Brothers, and two British institutions, the Household Mortgage Corporation and the National Home Loans Corporation are looking to the development of a secondary market in mortgages, such as exists in the USA, to enable them to expand further into the market.

While retail banking may be subjected to competition from a variety of sources it might be thought by the big banks that their corporate business remains safe. However, with bankruptcies at record levels, and banks' bad debt provisions in the last year for UK borrowers at over £500 million – up, as the Deputy Governor of the Bank of England noted, choosing his base point acidly, 'from a negligible amount in 1979 to an amount equivalent to a quarter of the pre-tax profits [in 1984]' – this is not perhaps unadulteratedly good news.

In fact it seems that competition to banks is coming from bank customers themselves and is a matter of some irritation as well as concern. The trend started many years ago in the US with the formation in the 1980s of the General Electric Credit Corporation, which now manages over $21 billion of the parent company's assets. British GEC have recently established their own quasi-banking financial subsidiary, headed by an ex-Rothschild man, to administer a £200 million portfolio and to develop new methods of credit for GEC industrial and governmental customers.

The most advanced British industrial in-house bank is BP Finance, an almost fully-fledged merchant bank, which in the current year is expected to produce profits at the level of £30 million. According to its chief executive, John Brown, BP Finance 'thinks like a bank', and is 'an all singing, all dancing, finance group'. As well as performing standard treasury operations, BP Finance acts as a foreign exchange trader, with a turnover of $100 billion a year, arranges funding for associate companies, has a capital markets group, and arranges long-term interest swaps, all with a staff of 110, including twelve traders. Its largest issue to date has been a $6.5 billion credit, for itself, managed by itself.

The logic behind such operations is impeccable, but it is easy to see how much of the most profitable part of a bank's business can be sliced away from underneath by its own customers.

A further tranche of the clearing banks' traditional markets will disappear if a sterling commercial paper market develops. British companies already borrow short term directly rather than through banks in US dollars as part of the existing American market. Notes are issued for very short periods – the average US maturity is only twenty-two days – but the market is huge: some $260 billion.

At present it is illegal under the Banking Act to issue sterling commercial paper under one year, but it is likely that this will be extended to enable British companies to find their short-term requirements directly. Only the biggest and most secure of companies will participate in this market, but it is exactly these companies who now make use of the very considerable sums on overdraft.

We have seen how British brokers neglected the new markets that developed in the 1970s: there is every indication that British banks were equally slow.

After the revelations of the Third-World loan exposure and the troubles of Continental Illinois in 1982 even the largest American banks suffered damage to their credit rating. This is, in the US, not a matter of wine-bar gossip but of ascertainable fact. Both Moody's and Standard & Poor's credit rating agencies publish ratings of corporate credit, which at that time showed the banks dropping below, sometimes well below, the assessments of their main customers. It therefore became impossible for such customers to raise money at finer rates direct from the market by issuing their own paper. The move was welcomed by investors with great enthusiasm; not only AAA companies but ones with much less credibility found that they could profitably borrow in this market. The Walt Disney Corporation, for example, a company of only modest size by US standards, but known to everyone, was able to launch a successful $75 million issue at a rate well below that which would have been provided by the banks.

This business is market-led: that is, investment bankers know what will attract investors and can package issues accordingly. Perhaps for this very reason note issues have so far been strikingly more successful than syndicated bank loans; note investors turn up their noses at projects and countries that banks fall over themselves to finance. The role of the bigger banks is now limited to granting the back-up facilities, which they are happy enough to do since these form only contingent liabilities which do not appear on their balance sheets.

The extent to which British institutions have failed to gain strong positions in the Euromarkets was indicated in a poll carried out by Euromoney. Leading Euromarket borrowers were asked, 'Which bank is the most professional, overall, in arranging a facility in the international capital markets?' No British banks appeared in the top ten: Morgan Grenfell and Warburg, together with the consortium bank Orion Royal, were in the next ten. The big banks were nowhere.

It is probably by now too late for the big banks to do much about breaking into the Euronote market: they should be looking to the next development. A timely warning was given by the Deputy Governor of the Bank of England in September 1985 at a conference in Lausanne against the perils of attempting business which one did not fully understand:

A strategy of diversification, then, while it may seem an obvious way to compensate for a shrinking demand for the 'core' business of lending, needs to be weighed carefully against its possible costs. A well-thought-out decision to diversify away from lending into other clearly defined areas of business may indeed by a sensible way forward for some international banks – but perhaps not for all. Certainly it is no guarantee of higher returns simply to imitate those who have for many years been making their living by providing these different financial services, or to adopt a haphazard approach to diversification in the hope that the various activities will somehow be mutually reinforcing ...

Expertise must be acquired, either by recruiting qualified and experienced staff or by gaining experience gradually in the market place. There are all too many precedents for banks getting into difficulties by internal diversification at too rapid a pace, failing to appreciate the hazards of the new activity.

Another warning came from a Bank executive director, Peter Cooke, whose Basle committee has begun work on how financial innovation, which it describes rather confusingly as 'of the order of magnitude of significance to the original development of the euromarkets', can be monitored; and a worrying analysis it is. 'Some of these [techniques] are technically very complicated and are probably only fully understood by a small number of traders and market experts.' Traders are never the aptest of communicators (as anyone who has seen outside directors of banks trying to understand what the Treasury director is going on about can confirm), yet they have to be able to commit their houses to very large sums indeed.

Suspicions are expressed by the committee that some banks lack 'a sound grasp of the risk involved in options trading', which can be a particularly dangerous field, exhibiting great volatility; funding risks implicit in underwriting commitments, undrawn loan and overdraft facilities, standby letters of credit, are easier to identify and control but very large in total, and at the moment not reflected in any way in a bank's balance sheets.

The Bank of England has suggested that these should be calculated at 50 per cent of a standard loan in calculating capital requirements; the FED (the Federal Reserve Bank) have made a series of proposals which, if adopted, would even further aggravate Third-World difficulties. These suggestions involve weighting loans according to perceived and arbitrary standards. At present all loans, including sovereign risk and bank loans, except those in trouble, are assessed as a standard risk: exceptions proposed are that cross-border loans to industrialized countries and banks would carry a 60 per cent weighting, and claims on US banks and loan commitments would only have a 30 per cent risk weighting – which compares to the Bank of England's proposed 50 per cent. If American banks have to differentiate between good (Western) and less good (Developing World) governments and banks there can be little doubt what they will do.

Among the merchant banks the Accepting Houses Committee will be a casualty of the revolution, although in fact it has been of little practical significance for some years. There is no community of interest between such small idiosyncratic houses as Rea Brothers on the one hand and Kleinwort and Hambros on the other, just as there is little difference between Brown Shipley (inside) and Leopold Joseph (out).

Some of the accepting houses are so small as to be negligible, and even the most substantial hardly compare in size with their American competitors (see table 10). In some work this is not important; a small bank can do as well as the biggest in takeovers and mergers, if it has the right man, but capital is vital in international business.

Table 10 Equity and capital of American and British Investment Banks

	1984			
	£ million			*$ million*
Kleinwort	215	Merrill Lynch		1,888
Warburg	140	Salomon		1,181
Schroder	125	Dean Witter		961
Hill Samuel	123	Shearson		710
Morgan Grenfell	116			

Annual Reports

A survey made by Databank predicted that only Kleinwort, Warburg and Morgan would survive as a 'one-stop' traditional merchant bank and that all others will have to find specialist niches, as some, like Robert Fleming, have already done, becoming what is currently described as a 'boutique' using the talents of those with individual interests who dislike larger organizations.

The discount houses are also a dying species, now reduced to five independent firms and due to be replaced by an extraordinary collection of no fewer than twenty-nine gilt 'market makers', six 'inter dealer brokers' and nine Stock Exchange money brokers. How many of these institutions survive is an interesting question, considering that the much larger New York market, trading 35,000 different securities and turning over $100 billion, supports fewer firms, while London will be handling at most 150 stocks with a daily turnover of £1 billion.

Many of the gilt market traders are going to operate on a cottage industry scale, while at the other end of the scale Barclays are installing 600 trading positions, Kleinworts 350, and Mercury (Warburg) 465. Citicorp is taking the whole of the old Billingsgate market, thus spawning a generation of fishy jokes.

The perils facing the new ventures are twofold; they may lack the capital needed to stand a run of difficulties, or their new systems may not work. A sample of the latter was given in 1985 when the Bank of New York's computer decided to accept orders, pay for them, but refrain from collecting the money due to the bank. Nobody could stop the insanely generous machine for nearly 24 hours, during which it paid out nearly

$30 billion. Murphy's law must surely dictate that at least one British computer will do likewise, and the resulting chaos could be devastating.

Human nature is, however, more reliable than machines. Faced with such massive overcapacity, thousands of dealers and brokers are going to be scrabbling in the markets for what they can get in order to justify the fees they have been paid and the investments made in housing them. Some will cheat. The complexities of the system and the untried regulatory bodies mean that some will be able to go on cheating for a long time, enough to pile up unmanageable losses. Some firms will go broke. Imaginative market men will invent ever more fascinating instruments (although no one is likely to do better than that splendid Scots adventurer who invented a new state, the Kingdom of Poyais in Central America, with himself as king, and attempted to raise loans in the London market). Some will sail too close to the wind, and predictable disaster will follow in the wake of the first serious bear market.

High among the list of the most unpopular jobs in the country will be membership of the regulatory bodies. In the inexorable nature of these things three classes of persons will join or be drafted: the gifted, who do it out of a sense of duty but whose heart is back in their own businesses; the deadbeats, pushed out of the way by their firms, and the professional committee men. With luck there will always be some tough and dedicated characters like Kenneth Berrill willing to steer their boards for the sake of the reputation of the City.

PART SIX
The Big Bang

14

The Big Bang

In the early months of 1975 Wall Street existed in a state of acute anxiety and apprehension. The consumption of lunchtime Martinis tripled as investment bankers, dealers and brokers talked in apocalyptic tones of Mayday: all were convinced that Mayday would bring the destruction, not only of the New York Stock Exchange, but that of 'the other Exchanges in the country; create confusion and chaos in the market of securities ... destroy our capital-raising mechanism, and bring about the downfall of our free enterprise system.'

Mayday was not some revolutionary strategem, nor an international emergency call, although both these overtones were heavily stressed, but the coming about of free competition in this bastion of free enterprise. On 1 May 1975 fixed commissions on security dealings were abolished, and brokers were allowed to strike their own bargains with their customers.

Pretty obviously none of these dire prognostications were fulfilled, since the New York Stock Exchange has since flourished exceedingly: had Mayday not taken place, according to one commentator, 'In a few years there would have been no business on the Exchange in large institutional trading'. In much the same way a little honest competition is not likely to do anything but good to the London Stock Exchange when its Big Bang takes place on 27 October 1986: the dangers that may be expected, which are real enough, spring from other causes than the incursion of competition between brokers.

It was indeed the lack of such competition, enshrined in the restrictive practices of the Stock Exchange, that touched off a movement which has now advanced much further, and promises to dethrone the Stock Exchange from its present eminence to the level of but one of a number of regulatory agencies all subject to a single supervisory authority.

Like Mayday, the Big Bang is concerned with the abolition of minimum and fixed commissions charged by brokers, but it would be misleading if the term were taken to refer only to the comparatively minor events scheduled to occur in October 1986. The City will not awake on the 28th to find itself a changed place; not even the Stock Exchange will be overwhelmed by investors determined to negotiate new rate of commissions, having stored up a vast backlog of business against the opportunity. The 1986 Budget reduction in stamp duty from 1 per cent to half per cent alone will have a more significant effect, and the change in rules governing the control of brokers and jobbers, hitherto required to be independent but allowed to be completely owned by outside organizations, will change the whole character of the institution.

The Big Bang might be more aptly defined as a series of more-or-less-controlled explosions, the cumulative effect of which will amount to a transformation. The City of the future will see no more of many familiar institutions: stockbrokers and jobbers are being acquired by banking and investment groups; the accepting houses are fragmented in interest, and their erstwhile distinction has become meaningless; the discount houses' traditional function will be absorbed in a new gilts market; and the London Metal Exchange is transforming its old practices. These fundamental changes can justify to the hilt the sobriquet of the 'Big Bang'. No longer parochial the City of London is becoming international: its future is not that of a group of time-honoured and time-worn institutions but as one of the world's 'mega-centres' of finance along with Tokyo and New York. The alterations in the rules of the Stock Exchange are only one symptom of a more fundamental change.

The Stock Exchange lacks these qualities of individuality and style that both Lloyd's and the Bank of England undoubtedly possess. Every country with claims to a market economy has its Stock Exchange, often indeed several, and that of London is neither the oldest nor the biggest. For the first century of its history the activities of the Stock Exchange were confined almost entirely to dealing in government securities, and later in foreign stocks and shares. British industrial and commercial enterprises drew their financial resources from private capital and short term bank finance until after the First World War, when the growing size of companies formed by post-war mergers led to a demand for access to public rather than private finance.

Until recent years the Stock Exchange has still not provided as much in the way of finance for industry as similar institutions have done in other countries. A discordant chorus of blame arises when this subject is mentioned. Those who make it their business to provide capital – banks, insurance companies, and the Stock Exchange itself – protest their willingness, even their anxiety, to make copious flows of cash available while pension funds complain of their inability to find stocks in which to invest their burgeoning funds: it is industry, they say, that refuses to ask for them. Industrialists for their part object that unlike their competitors abroad they cannot borrow long term from their bankers: should they seek a public quotation, they will make themselves subject to endless aggravations from small shareholders, suffer restrictions on their freedom of movement and, more importantly, be forced to concentrate on short-term profitability.

The complaints are less justified today than they might have been even ten years ago. In 1974 I participated in one of the first term-loans to be made to industry, where lending was monitored by a series of performance ratios, agreed after mutual analysis of the borrower's needs and prospects. As long as the company observed these ratios the loan continued in its original form; their infraction gave the lender the right to call or re-negotiate the loan. Since that time institutions have become both readier and better equipped to join with companies in evolving corporate plans and thereby ensuring access to capital markets.

These developments are comparatively new. In 1960-65 UK domestic issues on the capital market as a proportion of GNP were lower than in any other major country except Greece. In 1971 the Governor of the Bank of England reminded investors that 'in terms of actual volume of funds raised by new capital issues, there is no ground whatsoever for complacency. In proportion to national income, the amounts raised on new capital issues by domestic borrowers (excluding government issues) has been lower in the UK than in the EEC on the average of the last five years; considerably lower, not much more than half the level,' (quoted in *Capital City*, McRae and Cairncross).

Some of the blame for this state of things must attach to the Stock Exchange's adhesion to its own comfortable restrictive practices and reluctance to attempt innovation; a situation much analogous to that pertaining at the same time among the clearing banks.

The peculiar institution of the London Stock Exchange is that known as 'single capacity', or the broker-jobber system. Anyone wanting to buy or sell stocks or shares approaches a stockbroker, who then acts as his agent in a negotiation with a 'jobber'. The broker himself takes no risk, except that of his client defaulting, and employs no capital. He is the contact man *par excellence*, traditionally equipped with a repertoire of lubricious jokes and exuding *bonhomie*. Jobbers look upon themselves as decidedly superior; a jobber takes a position in those shares in which he deals, and is able to quote prices for buying and selling. In theory this means that competition between the jobbers should ensure that the margin of profit is restricted, and that the broker can obtain the best price for his client. The jobber after all does not intend to make offers to the public, nor the broker to deal except through jobbers.

The system did not prove capable of expanding with the market. Although the number of jobbers shrank from over a hundred after the war to only thirteen in 1979 (of which five shared 90 per cent of the market) even the largest of these lacked sufficient capital or access to credit to enable them to hold stock in quantities sufficient to match increasingly large demands. The whole jobbing community could deploy a combined capital of less than £100 million to serve a market with a turnover of several thousand million. Brokers were less seriously affected: they needed only modest capital resources; enough to maintain an office and to finance any unexpected hiccups and after all, servicing capital only swallowed up profits that might otherwise be distributed among the partners.

The shape of the market itself did not help: although more securities are quoted on the London Stock Exchange than on the New York Exchange, London has an uneven mix ranging from very small companies to some of the largest in the world; a system to suit both was impossible, and in recent years the larger British companies' shares have increasingly been traded abroad.

Whether as a result of the protective system and the lethargy it engendered, or because of the restrictive regulations placed on the market by the Labour governments between 1974 and 1979, the developing world of finance bypassed the Stock Exchange almost entirely. Exchange controls limited British investors' access to foreign, especially American, markets. The dollar premium made investment for any but the dedicated unattractive, and British brokers made little effort to develop expertise in these matters. Innovations such as traded options were rejected, often with contumely. Over-the-counter markets, which enabled companies too small or risky to fulfil Stock Exchange requirements, a service essential to expanding industries, developed outside the aegis of the Stock Exchange.

Even more seriously the Stock Exchange missed out on the expansion of Euro-security business that followed the removal of United States restrictions in 1974. At first most of this was absorbed by the banks' issues of Eurocurrency loans, but when the Third-World debt problems began to surface in 1981 and the loan market shrivelled, negotiable bonds shot into prominence.

In the last five years Eurobonds and their siblings have become the most important part of the securities market and are available in bewildering prolixity. They may be nominated in US dollars, Deutschmarks, sterling, yen, Swiss francs, Australian or New Zealand dollars, Ecus or mixed currencies. They may carry fixed interest, floating interest, or no interest at all (but with a suitably enhanced repayment value), and be issued at par, at premium, or discount: they may offer conversion facilities, or carry warrants. They are freely marketable and transferable, and can be held anywhere without the inconvenience of notifying revenue authorities.

Issuers vie with one another in the ingenuity they apply to creating new investment opportunity. Profits can be spectacular; in 1985 Électricité de France launched a Eurodollar floating rate note with one year warrants to buy a fixed rate Ecu bond with a nine and three-quarter per cent coupon. The fall of the dollar and the rise of the Ecu effected a rise in the value of the warrants during the year from $14 to $200.

All of this is highly remunerative business has by-passed the Stock Exchange and is carried out by a variety of brokerage houses. At present a dealer in securities can legally operate in at least ten different ways. He may be a member of the Stock Exchange, or among the six hundred licensed dealers by the Department of Industry under the Prevention of Fraud (Investments) Act, or belong to one of the eight associations of dealers recognized by the Department of Trade and Industry, mainly groups of foreign houses. The Prevention of Fraud Act also allows some 350 banks, quasi-banks and insurance companies to deal in securities. They are however asked to conduct the majority of their business through either a Stock Exchange or licensed dealer.

Such a system presents obvious regulatory difficulties. A succession of scandals were brought to public attention in the early 1980s of which the most painful, affecting as it did some of the Bank of England staff's own money, was the collapse of Norton Warburg, a firm outside the jurisdiction of either the Stock Exchange or the Bank of England in 1981: over £4 million was missing. At the same time, after a long investigation by the Fraud Squad, the papers concerning the Piccadilly Unit Trust went to the Director of Public Prosecutions; Christopher Moran took an unsuccessful libel action against a newspaper which had suggested that he had been a party to certain reinsurance transactions; most seriously, a number of unpleasantnesses in the silver futures market, taken together, gave a shabby air to much of the City's transactions.

Even the Stock Exchange had one of its scandals, when in 1982 six members were expelled following the Halliday Simpson affair, an uncharacteristic episode, since in its own dealings with the public the London Stock Exchange has maintained high standards of integrity. Stockbrokers may have earned an easy living, but they have done so without defrauding their clients. The machinery is well-tested; all complaints are investigated, and the Exchange's surveillance department may make its own investigations as it chooses.

Allegations of impropriety are investigated by the disciplinary committee of the council and the results published. Some matters are only minor infringements, as in the case of Mr X who was censured for the following offence:

Mr X was told that he should take dealing instructions from a person who would be known to him only as 'Chris'. He never asked 'Chris' for his full name or address, or why he should not be apprised of his identity.

Although there was no evidence that Mr X was aware of the fact at the time, it transpired that 'Chris' was an employee of another member firm.

Mr X was found to have acted in a disgraceful manner by accepting dealing instructions from an employee of a member firm other than his own without proper enquiries – which he could and should have made – as to the full name and identity of that employee.

A certain account was maintained in a fictitious name, and Mr X either knew the identity of the client or, by failing to make proper enquiries, wilfully closed his eyes to the position. By withholding from or misrepresenting to his firm the identity of the client responsible for this account he acted contrary to the provisions of Rule 84(2)(e).

A far cry from the PCW affair at Lloyd's, it might be thought! More serious misdemeanours are energetically investigated and severely punished, but these are few and far between. As far as the mechanics of dealing are concerned it is difficult to fault the record of the Stock Exchange as its own regulatory body. The major difficulties lie outside the community in Old Broad Street, particularly in the matters of insider dealing and takeover bids.

The Westland affair afforded an example in 1985/6. This bitterly fought engagement between a group of European investors and Sikorsky/Fiat for control of the British helicopter company, which resulted in the resignation of two cabinet ministers and the reported attempt to bribe the opposition in the shape of Alan Bristow, was resolved after a period of frantic dealing during which blocks of shares changed hands at prices well above those obtainable in the market. This was done by means of 'put throughs' or special deals in which potential buyers of large amounts of stock were matched with sellers and prices agreed far in excess of those available to other shareholders. Some 20 per cent of the total stock ended up in six mystery accounts, including three Swiss bank nominees, the holders of which all voted in favour of the American offer, which was also that supported by the UK government and the Westland board.

The Takeover Panel did not feel that it could use its powers to intervene, since no regulations were obviously being broken, but at least one senior official there was privately outspoken, saying to me that what went on in Westminster made the City 'look like the City of God'. The matter was referred instead, after the event, to the council of the Stock Exchange, which completed its report in April 1986. Since there had been no rules broken, because none were formulated, the disciplinary committee of the council was not involved, and the main recommendation was that a committee should be established to formulate such rules. Such an anodyne outcome might have been acceptable had not the Stock Exchange council accompanied the announcement of the completion and acceptance of its report with another refusing to publish it, since by publication it was believed that the council might expose itself to being sued for libel. The committee of investigation made the bounds of its own credulity apparent when they said, as reported in the *Financial Times* of 3 April 1986:

> It is difficult to credit that overseas buyers should consider it worth their while to pay much more than the company's worth without some collaboration with one or the other parties.
>
> It is not beyond the bounds of possibility that there are six ingenuous foreigners in the world, but the committee's credibility was sufficiently stretched to be sceptical as to the absence of such a concert party.
>
> In the absence of hard evidence, the committee says, however, that it is unable to prove the existence of a concert party. The case was therefore dropped.

The Stock Exchange might wring its collective hands over such goings on, and comfort itself with the thought that this fiasco was the government's responsibility and that otherwise no finger of accusation could credibly be pointed at the Exchange, whose rules were well observed and where decency prevailed. In truth the institution had been dying of inanition, having achieved order at the expense of avoiding evolution.

Although the Stock Exchange still possesses a massive physical presence in the City, its 23-storey tower overshadowing the neighbouring Bank of England, the Royal Exchange and the Mansion House, the institution housed in this majestic pile has rapidly diminished in importance. It may be that allowing negotiated commissions would have done something to stop the rot, but the complacent self-satisfaction that inspired the Exchange to propose an increase in commissions as late as 1982 at a time when it was the subject of a Court Action under the Restrictive Practices Act, was hubristic.

Hubris has been encouraged by a series of events which in the nature of things cannot be repeated. The sale of public assets that was pursued by Convervative governments from 1980 may have some justification in terms of public policy, but it certainly brought enormous profits to the City. Apart from a slip at the issue of Britoil, which was mistakenly overpriced, issue after issue has been made at substantial discounts to market prices showing profits to successful stags, and, whether successful or not, making very substantial fee incomes for brokers and advisers.

The British Telecom issue was the most notorious, and has been severely criticized by the Audit Committee. Apart from the initial underpricing which rendered the issue the most lavish governmental gift since the

Roman Empire cut back on bread and circuses (and the excuses about the difficulty of getting the market right should be treated with the incredulity they deserve: what are brokers and bankers paid for?) The powerful selling campaign and unprecedently generous distribution of sales commissions were enough to have sold a much less attractive stock.

It was fortunate for stockbrokers that these strokes of good fortune came at exactly the right time for their profits to be maximized.

In 1983 the chairman of the Stock Exchange, Sir Nicholas Goodison, managed to agree with Cecil Parkinson, during the latter's brief tenure of office at the Department of Trade and Industry, that the Restrictive Practices case against the Stock Exchange would be dropped on condition that the latter agreed a number of reforms, including the abolition of minimum commissions, which had to be introduced by the end of 1986. One of the reforms was the agreement to allow participation by outsiders in Stock Exchange firms. At first limited to 29.9 per cent, it was accepted that full ownership would eventually be allowed, and that this would inevitably lead to most, if not all, of the existing firms becoming swallowed up in larger groupings. The terms on which this could be done would naturally reflect the most recent earnings of the Stock Exchange firms, and would therefore ensure high prices.

Negotiations on the mergers started in 1983 and were largely complete by 1985. As banks bought into the new markets it was clear that, for better or for worse, the City would never be the same again.

Those engaging themselves in the business of stockbroking who enjoyed the benefits of a classical education, a dwindling number, reflect that not since Danae enjoyed the favours of Zeus had a shower of gold descended to the earth with such agreeable fecundity as occurred in the *annus mirabilis* of 1985. The fruit of that descent was no hero, but an influx of new motor cars, country houses, hunters and yachts as banks fell over themselves in their eagerness to buy up stockbroking partnerships.

As the purchase of Crocker by Midland and Grindlays by the ANZ demonstrate, few things are more insatiable than a bank determined on making an acquisition. It is true that measuring the value of a partnership with little in the way of capital or tangible assets with any precision is difficult. Such fixed assets as there may be are of minimal importance; what is offered is income, historic and projected, flowing from the ability of those individuals in post to create it. Purchasers erred on the side of generosity.

The process spawned a collection of nomenclatures as purchases attempted to secure the continuing services of these acolytes: golden handshakes were things of the past; the talk was now of golden hellos, golden farewells, golden handcuffs, golden parachutes, and of the unfortunate marzipan men – those who found themselves below the icing.

Problems are inevitably arising with differences between the treatment of existing banking staff and those in the new financial services companies. Barclays, for instance, found it necessary to designate nearly one quarter of the total Wedd Durlacher staff as partners in their new joint trading concern, with a right to share in profits. Several of these could – and there will be many junior staff among them – earn a great deal more than a senior branch bank manager.

Mark Weedon, of Egon Zehnder, estimates that the head of sales and trading in even a medium-sized house can expect to earn more than £200,000 a year, and sometimes much more, and that even quite junior dealers, responsible for no staff but only for their own activities, can top £100,000. I know of at least one dealer grossing a quarter of a million. Even these sums are modest by comparison with what can be earned in the US or Japan, and there is little to prevent dealers from operating in these markets as easily as in London. All international banking business is carried out in English, and dealing is a skill that transcends every frontier. Any trading floor, even in France, is likely to house dealers of half-a-dozen nationalities.

Salaries of such impressive magnitude dwarf what is available in clearing banks. The Midland, for example, reported in 1984 that from a total workforce of more than 80,000 no employee and only six directors earned

Table 11 Comparative academic and City salaries

Post	Age and qualifications	Salary scale
Research assistant	Hons maths/physics	£5,900
Post doc. fellowship	PhD science 29–30	£10,000–12,000
Research fellowship	Post doc. experience 30+	£9,000–11,500
Lectureship in computer studies	Maths/engineering Hons, teaching experience 25+	£8,000–15,000
Glaxo research assistant	PhD microbiology 25+	£13,160
Accountant	Under 30 tax specialist	£25,000
Bank: general	2 years' experience merchant bank, mid 20s, maths background	£20,000
Fund manager	Accountancy qualifications 30+	£30,000*
Finance manager, merchant bank	Graduate with 3 years' experience corporate finance	£30,000*
Financial planner	Accountancy 30–35	£33,000–38,000
Internal auditor	Accountancy 28–35	£22,000*

*plus bonuses

more than £70,000 a year in the UK – enough perhaps to buy a 23-year-old dealer with a couple of years' experience. Another thirty-nine employees and directors earned between £45,000 and £70,000: very few if any of these can have been managers of even large branches, since most of the highest rewards are gained in head offices or regional head offices. There are, for example, some thirty of general manager rank.

Bank staffs are growing restive under what is seen to be gross unfairness; even the Bank of England Staff Association, which must rank among the least revolutionary section of organized labour, has been moved to protest.

In the course of the run up to the Big Bang I acted as chairman at two conferences arranged by the Institute for International Research in London. Both were well attended by representatives of all types of financial institutions, and at both concern that the City was gaining a reputation for unbridled greed was manifest.

Outside the City this sort of thing looks distastefully absurd. It is interesting, for example, to compare the 'situations vacant' advertised in the *Financial Times* with those in the *New Scientist*, bearing in mind that while all academic positions must be advertised, only the least attractive and more junior of the financial apppointments are made in this way, the better ones being filled on a personal basis.

In any terms that might be employed other than the crudest of saloon-bar economics the importance to society of research workers must at least equal that of market traders. Other arguments might be advanced to justify an imbalance (although hardly that of security of tenure, since research workers have not more certainty of the future than the most highly geared dealer) but lack force in the face of such monstrous disparity.

The City establishment was well seized of the argument; comments were prompted such as those made by John Quinton, a deputy director of Barclays, who attacked those who, by incompetence or greed as well as those who made sweeping and careless condemnations, 'damaged the reputation of the City', and insisted that regulation must be even more effective.

Sir Timothy Bevan, chairman of Barclays, had previously asked for restraint, saying that it was 'embarrassing for us who live here', and that the City 'was subject to a lot of political and social opprobrium for paying what is perceived generally as too much'.

These reactions – and the unsympathetic ones were much less elegantly expressed – coupled with the scandals that were being uncovered, created a climate of opinion near to that which prompted the establishment of the SEC – the Securities Exchange Commission of the United States – in 1933.

The SEC is an institution whose very name sends a thrill of horror through the City. If the horror was confined to the unrighteous no further discussion would be needed, but many of the most upright abominate the idea of a government commission, and make it worth investigating how far their fears may be justified.

15

SEC or SIB

There are few human activities that give keener delight than the formulation of rules; especially if it is intended that they should be observed by others. From the days of Leviticus and Deuteronomy to those of the Football Association the compilation of lists of what is prescribed and what proscribed, and the punishment of transgressors, has been a jealously guarded prerogative of rulers.

A few thousand years of bitter experience has done little to lessen the faith of those engaged in the governing of society that all can be made well if only we think up the right rules and make sure the other chaps stick to them. It is therefore hardly to be wondered at that Parliament is enthusiastic about the prospect of firm statutory regulation of the City, nor that those engaged in its daily business would prefer to settle things among themselves. Merchants have complained at least since 1681 that ''Tis well known of late years, the House of Commons has been filled with gentlemen, whose ignorance of and unconcern for trade has brought it to the condition it is now in.'

In order to take a reasonable view of the matter we need to remind ourselves of the purpose of the market. It is, as I see it, just as it was in the Middle Ages; the conditions under which trade will flourish are the same in an Afghan bazaar as in Lime Street. A market provides conditions in which trade may be safely and expeditiously carried out: it must provide protection for those who frequent it and obtain the observance of recognized standards of quality, but allow for innovation and development. Should a market not be seen to be accessible and secure it will decay; as did Lee Fair in West Yorkshire, which in 1656 had 'become a tumultuous meeting of the idle and loose persons of the country where there is much revelling and drunkenness. And hath been noted these many years to be a meeting where there is usually more or less bloodshed and some lives lost.' Bloodshed in the City streets is now rare, but it remains to the advantage of all there that their affairs should be subject to seemly regulation.

A balance, which has often been elusive, must therefore be sought between a control so tight that business is discouraged, and a free-for-all only frequented by the tumultuous and brazen.

One extreme might be that represented by Richard Minns, in his book *Take Over the City*, in which he claims that no controls can suffice and that all the financial services should be nationalized. A not dissimilar line is taken by Francis Cripps et al. in *Manifesto – a Radical Strategy for Britain's future*, which envisages wholesale expropriation with all exchange withering away and shares being exchanged 'for entitlements to future benefits on some progressive scale'. Fortunately this sort of theological nonsense appeals to few and certainly not to those members of the Labour Party whose latest (1982) study group of the City recommended proposals similar to those of Professor Gower which do not differ greatly from what is likely to be established.

The political view, whether from the left or right, focuses on investor protection. Professor Gower, who was asked by the government to report on this question, concluded that:

> When investors, individually or collectively through pension funds, venture into the financial markets, they enter a jungle where the rules are made and imposed by those who operate the markets. This reliance on non-statutory 'self-regulation' has, we believe, been shown to be inadequate to protect investors and has allowed serious conflicts of interest to develop.

Oddly enough, starting from an opposed viewpoint, the Labour Party study group's conclusions are the same.

> There should be a new Securities Act which would set up a new Securities Commission responsible for the supervision and control of the securities markets.
>
> The Act would define each individual activity covered (managing funds for third parties, broking, jobbing, underwriting, etc.) and all firms wishing to do business in any of these activities would be required to register with the Commission.
>
> In the case of certain activities (such as fund management), the Commision would not allow firms performing those activities to perform other activities where this might give rise to conflicts of interest. This would require substantial divestments by some financial institutions.
>
> The Act would recognize certain self-regulatory bodies whose constitution, rules and membership would be subject to supervision by the Securities Commission.

The danger of stressing the element of protection is that the fraud and deception might be avoided only at the cost of slowly strangling the market. The US has had painful experience of how this can take place, when in the 1960s the combination of a credit squeeze which held down interest rates and an insistence by the authorities on balances and capital controls, notably the Interest Equalization Tax, ensured that the enormously lucrative Eurodollar market was established outside the US.

This is not something that the UK can afford to risk. Ever since the industrial revolution the UK has had a favourable balance of trade in manufactured goods – or had at least until 1983 when for the first time the erstwhile workshop of the world imported £5,000 million more goods than she exported. By 1984 this deficit had grown to £6,200 million, and shows little sign of improving (see table 12). We have paid our way by invisible exports, tourism and the financial services industries, which in 1985 earned some £8 billion. Even here there are worrying signs that London may be losing its position as a world financial centre. Consider the decline of the pound sterling as an international currency.

Table 12 Decline of sterling

1 Percentage of nations denominating reserves in

	1974	1984
US$	75	57
Sterling	5.4	2.6
D-Mark	5.8	11.0

2 International bank lending, 1985

	US$ bn
US	210.9
D-Mark	48.7
Swiss Franc	14.8
Ecu (European Currency Unit)	6.0
Yen	3.0
£	2.8
French Franc	1.8

Safeguarding the future of these golden eggs is therefore a matter of prime importance, and it is well known that geese lay better when not disturbed.

For such apparently good reasons the City has been suspicious of anything that resembles the level of control experienced in the USA. It is not so clear that the City is justified in its suspicions, and it is interesting to take an unprejudiced look at the matter.

The United States economy is the most prosperous, and its markets the largest, in the world; it would be odd if these were incompetently run. A major current distinction is that two sets of regulatory agency exist in the US, the Federal Reserve Bank overseeing the affairs of the banks, and the

Securities Exchange Commission those of the securities industry, much the same system as proposed in the UK with the exception that the SEC is a statutory organization of the sort that the City wants our own Securities and Investment Board not to be. But the SEC came into being as a result of disquiet over banking misbehaviour, twenty years after the establishment of the Federal Reserve, which had proved itself powerless to intervene. The SEC therefore exerts over all companies which offer securities in the market, including banks, a similar statutory control to that which the Bank of England has itself effectively exercised over banks.

The techniques of British central bank control grew, as we have seen, from the quarter century of Montagu Norman's rule that carried the system through one world war and the aftermath of its predecessor. In spite of Norman's personal qualities this would hardly have been possible without the consistent willingness of both successive governments and the banks themselves to let him do it, facilitated by the geographical closeness of banks, controllers and government. In the US, controls were the product of a dramatic piece of politics.

Britain had not escaped the great Depression, with 3 million unemployed, but it did avoid anything as dramatic as the great Wall Street crash, when between September 1929 and July 1932 the value of securities quoted on the New York Stock Exchange fell from $90 billion to $16 billion. Our escape was due in part to the relative absence in London of the dangerous practice of buying shares on credit, which in a bear market can lead to a swiftly escalating loss, and in part to the unconscious Keynesianism of the population.

> English people were not too poor to lend abroad; they merely did not want to do so. An Englishman who put his money into tin mines, Argentine rails, or foreign government-bonds in the 1920s found himself in the 1930s with a stack of worthless, highly decorative share-certificates. An Englishman who built a fine modern house found himself with a fine modern house. (A.J.P. Taylor, *English History 1914-45*.)

American investors had however put a great deal of their money into highly decorative paper – their appetite for so doing was catered for, quite naturally, by American bankers, who searched out some very doubtful deals. In spite of consistently discouraging reports from their overseas offices ('Peru is ... careless in fulfilment of moral obligations ... frequent unobservance of undertakings ... flagrant disregard of guarantees ... long history of bond defaults') the National City Bank and J.W. Seligman organized $100 million of Peruvian bonds in 1927 and 1928 and sold the lot. No mention was made in the prospectus of the information they had received, and past defaults were glossed over.

As might be expected, by 1931 the bonds were worth between 6 and 25 per cent of their face value. To make matters worse these securities appeared to have the backing of the US government, since it was a requirement that any bank seeking to issue foreign stock should obtain the prior approval of the State Department. In fact this was automatically given, being a mere rubber stamp, but enabled the bonds to be marketed as having US government backing. As a result, between 1926 and 1930 American investors bought over $6 billion of foreign bonds.

President Hoover was worried about such goings on, but being a Republican, and tender of the susceptibilities of Wall Street, contented himself with worried mutterings, maintaining that 'it was doubtful whether there was constitutional authority for Federal regulation of the sale of securities'.

Roosevelt was made of different stuff; it is often forgotten that in his celebrated speech in which he swore, 'I pledge you, I pledge myself, to a new deal for the American people' he devoted the rest of the oration to 'the dry subject of finance', and made the promise of 'letting in the light of day on issues of securities, foreign and domestic, which are offered for sale to the investing public'.

One of the first acts of his new administration was to organize the Senate Banking Committee to set up a 'bear hunt'. The evidence produced to the committee shocked and embittered the American public. Fiorello La Guardia turned up with a trunkful of documents proving that a newspaper columnist, one Newton Plummer, had made himself more than a quarter of a million dollars by running share stories in newspapers, including the *New York Times* and the *Wall Street Journal*. Seligmans were revealed as having paid a price of $415,000 to Juan Leguia, the son of the Peruvian President, in order not to impede a bond issue they were making: an issue on which the bank received a commission of $4.5 million.

Chase had given in 1929 a personal loan of $200,000 to President Machado of Cuba, 'a dictator with a marked predisposition toward murder', as Professor Galbraith described him, and had employed the President's son.

The most distinguished banker of this time, Charles E. Mitchell of National City Bank, 'the representative banker of his generation ... who ... transformed commercial banking ... the genuis of the New Economic Era', was hauled before the committee and, within ten minutes, broken. He admitted that a fund had been established which absorbed 20 per cent of the bank's profits to be shared, at their own discretion, among senior executives. From this he had himself in 1927 and 1928 received over one million dollars; in 1929, at the height of the Depression, he had benefited by participation in an interest-free $2 million loan made by his own bank to their executives 'as a morale loan fund'. As late as 1933 only 5 per cent of this generous advance had been repaid. This was at a time when federal employees on a salary of $1,600 were being pressed to take a reduction.

Reaction was understandably bitter. Senator Carter Glass of Virginia, the acknowledged expert on banking law, who had been primarily responsible for preparing the Federal Reserve legislation, gave voice to the public view of bankers: 'One banker in my state attempted to marry a white woman and they lynched him'.

It is not difficult to be struck by certain similarities between the USA in the 1930s and Britain in the 1950s: Latin American debt, carelessly if not unscrupulously engaged, dubious commercial practices and extraordinarily high rewards at a period of national distress, and suspicion in the minds of the public of strange goings on in the financial community.

The establishment of the SEC was not greeted with unmixed enthusiasm. The *New York Times* called it 'autocratic meddling' and the *Wall Street Journal* warned of moves towards socialism, but both journals were feeling a little raw, and such feelings dispersed with the commission's success: by 1940 *Fortune* was calling its headquarters 'the chief memorial to a business era that came to an end ten years ago ... a shrine to the outraged feelings of the voters of 1932'.

Much of the SEC's power is due to its structure: it is not responsible to either the Federal Trade Commission or the Federal Reserve Board, who discharge functions broadly analogous to those of the Department of Trade and Industry, and the Bank of England, but is independent, its five members being appointed by the President for a fixed term and being removable only by Congress. Not more than three of its members must come from the same political partly, although the chairman usually finds himself in sympathy with the aims of the current administration. Joseph Kennedy was the somewhat unlikely first chairman, who saw his prime task as being that of restoring confidence in the capital markets rather than pursuing the more eye-catching of the past sinners, although more than two thousand cases of possible fraud were investigated. He was quickly successful in re-establishing a market: in 1935 $2.7 billion was raised on the market, more than four times the total of the previous year.

Although possessing wide powers, the SEC has successfully avoided becoming a Federal gunslinger, relying to an increasing extent on acts of persuasion. Stanley Sporken, whose indignation was aroused during the Watergate investigations by the revelation of the corporation's 'slush funds', encouraged firms to conduct their own investigations, and eschewed litigation in favour of 'consent decrees' when the accused party, without admitting guilt, promises to behave properly in the future and to pay whatever costs and fines the court considers appropriate, which in some instances may be considerable.

153

An example of this is the recent case against insider dealings in the 1981 Santa Fé takeover. This was a straightforward uncontested takeover in which the Kuwait Petroleum Corporation acquired the company, whose shares were registered in the New York and Pacific Stock Exchanges. Almost immediately afterwards the sec brought an action against a Kuwaiti businessman, Faisal al Massoud al Fuhaia and other 'unknown' purchasers' alleging that they had, acting on inside information, bought shares prior to the sale. The other unknown purchasers had, as happened in the UK during the 1986 Westland bid, bought their shares through nominee Swiss bank accounts, relying on traditional Swiss secrecy. It did not work, since the sec pursued the matter right through the Swiss courts and succeeded in obtaining a ruling, approved later by the Swiss government, ordering the banks to release the names of the purchasers. It turned out that one of these was a director of Santa Fé, one Darius Keaton, alias Nadir Katur Mabrouk, who not only bought shares himself prior to the bid but tipped off some friends, who were able to make profits of up to 1300 per cent: Mr Keaton-Mabrouk was alleged to have made $3.5 million himself, and his eight associates agreed to surrender $7.8 million they had themselves acquired. They included an Englishman, Mr Hildebrand McCulloch (which I am assured is a real name), and the interior minister of Qatar, Sheik Khalid bin Hamad al Thani.

The gentlemen concerned denied the charges: a settlement was made out of court, under the consent decree procedure. The conclusion was said to be 'amicable', and that 'there was no evidence of personal wrong-doing against Sheik Khalid, as evidenced by documents filed with the Court'. The $7.8 million was paid into a special claims fund established to reimburse any investors who might have lost money in Santa Fé share trading.

It took more than four years to push through this complex case in American, Swiss, French and English courts; it must be doubted whether an institution less firmly based than the sec, or having less in the way of financial and human resources, could have found the weight to fight an issue of such magnitude, especially against the reluctance of Swiss institutions to disclose their clients' affairs.

The Securities Exchange Commission as now constituted has two basic responsibilities; to ensure that companies which offer their securities for sale file complete and accurate information with the commission and make this information available to investors, and to protect investors against misrepresentation and fraud. Its powers derive from the Securities Act of 1933 which enables the commission to make 'whatever rules or regulations [are] deemed necessary or appropriate in the public interest or for the protection of investors', and in the more than fifty years of its life a substantial code of practice has been built up.

At the same time the commission is not asked to do too much: unlike other US regulatory agencies which have to concern themselves with the responsibilities for issuing licences and franchises, regulating prices and the minutiae of trade, the Securities Exchange Commission could define its own boundaries. Possibly as a result, but certainly as a record in public bodies, the SEC has kept its numbers firmly under control: there were 1,800 staff before the Second World War and 2,100 today.

US companies are much more generous with information and responsive to shareholder pressure (a factor which is increased by the wide responsibilities of directors under US law and the ability, indeed the enthusiasm, of American lawyers to file shareholder suits on a contingency basis). Where advances have been made in British company laws towards fuller disclosures these have been in an American direction.

It may well be, and it is certainly claimed in some quarters, that American companies are not thereby less prone to fraudulent manipulation than British ones and that we have gone quite far enough in making information available to shareholders. This misses the point; it is quite probable that there is as much, or more, fraud in the US than in Britain, but the question should be how much more might there be in the absence of the SEC. For conditions in the USA are very different from those prevalent in the constricted and concentrated UK market.

All this is, of course, expensive. The SEC spends about $130 million a year, one third – say $40 million – on enforcement. The results are not easy to assess. In 1985 269 actions were brought; 98 were concluded, of which the SEC lost only 6, which would indicate a standard of preparation a good deal higher than that common in the UK, where the success rate is much lower – the number of cases brought is also, making allowances for the size of the market, creditable.

The London Stock Exchange, by contrast, spends about £500,000 a year on regulation and enforcement, and keeps a market at least as orderly as that of the USA. As a result of the Stock Exchange's monitoring, twelve members have been expelled and twenty-three censured in the last eight years; of these seven were involved in the Hedderwick affair. With insider dealing the position is less happy. In the last five years before 1980, when this activity became a crime, 177 cases were investigated: in only eight of these was action taken and the offender made to hand over his profits to charity, hardly the most savage of punishments. Since that date a direct comparison can be made with the SEC; there have been just two successful prosecutions in six years.

The greatest potential improvement lies in increasing the ability to take legal action successfully. The responsibility for doing this is that of the DPP, but this department is much criticized and enjoys less than total

155

public support; the two successful cases mentioned represented the only prosecutions out of more than a hundred passed on by the Stock Exchange.

Adherence to SEC codes would also have made the Johnson Matthey débâcle impossible, at least in the form in which it took place. No American trading company would be allowed to conceal the affairs of a subsidiary bank (indeed, it would not be allowed to own such a bank) in the wholesale fashion adopted by the Johnson Matthey board. British banks which, by reason of their American investments, submit reports to the SEC, must publish these reports to their British shareholders, and mightily informative they are.

One reason for the lack of enthusiasm shown in the City for SEC-style regulation is due to the difficulty of imagining a British government being prepared to entrust powers outside a department of state. Some Civil Servant would most certainly want to draw it within his ambit. This may be wrong: the Bank of England has successfully retained and even expanded its own authority; Lloyd's has got its own Bill, and it may be that the SIB (Securities and Investment Board) can establish its independence firmly enough to resist encroachment. Nor is it easy to see a government appointing a board which must include members of the opposition parties. Indeed the equivocal attitude of the Labour Party towards the City would place obstacles in the way of an institution the prime objective of which is to improve and perfect the operation of a free market.

But the Roosevelt formula works. The Tennessee Valley Authority, which has also survived political pressure for over half a century, has succeeded in transforming the prospects of an area almost as large as England, and avoided becoming the creature of any political party. It has an even more independent structure – three board members, also appointed by the President, and irremovable in their nine-year term.

As a footnote it should be said that one aspect of the SEC that deserves imitation is its function as an information bureau. The Washington headquarters hold copies of all prospectuses, reports and accounts going back ten years, which are available for inspection. Up to ten pages of photocopying are also supplied free of charge, and research can be carried out for a fee (there is also a good sandwich bar and a helpful library). Regional headquarters hold some information and will obtain whatever is wanted. And, in contrast to the exorbitant prices charged by HMSO, copies of all relevant acts are made available free of charge. Recent governments have indeed made the discovery of company information even more difficult. The most basic of services are available in London: a charge is made, accounts fetched (but not prospectuses) and little is available in the way of background information.

National psyches are scarred by different events. America was shocked by the violent reaction of British public opinion to the Libyan bombings, not understanding that memories of the blitz have rendered aerial bombardment peculiarly distressing in this country; the British have difficulty in comprehending the trauma of the Iran hostages and the deaths of the Beirut marines that sharpened an American desire for revenge on no matter whom.

As memories of the Depression and crash fade, American business has grown more impatient of the controls and restrictions imposed in order to prevent a recurrence of that event.

The British, still unable to get a drink in the afternoon since doing so might risk inebriation among women munition workers anxious to defeat the Kaiser (our absurd licensing laws were imposed under the Defence of the Realm Act passed during the First World War), are torn between a reluctance to allow government any more powers and a concern that fair play should be seen.

The desire for fair play perhaps explains the success that the Monopolies and Mergers Commission and the Department of Fair Trading have had in stimulating the reform of both the banking and securities industries. It was as a result of the Monopolies and Mergers Commission's action that the Gower study was initiated. Its report, which appeared at the beginning of 1984, was politely critical of existing practices and made some far-reaching proposals, not all of which were much welcomed by the City. Central to Professor Gower's recommendations was the establishment of a commission to administer a new Investor Protection Act; the alternative was to have such an act administered directly by the Department of Trade and Industry, which, with the memories of the 123-banks, was a clear non-starter. But nervousness of a commission that might act as forcefully as the American SEC, and a strong feeling in both the Stock Exchange and the Bank of England in favour of preserving their freedom of action, have led to a debate on the subject that has continued for more than two years. The Bank, which put together is own advisory team, convinced the Department that regulatory powers should be delegated to a private practitioner body, the Securities and Investment Board (SIB). The Stock Exchange, under the aegis of the new board, would continue to run its own affairs as it had done, quite successfully, previously, and non-Stock Exchange dealers would have to put together their own parallel bodies, reporting, like the Stock Exchange, to the SIB.

The proposed British organization followed the American pattern closely: a central board with general powers of oversight delegating responsibility for day-to-day control to the practitioners' own organizations – Stock Exchanges and other Associations of Dealers in Financial

Investments, generically known as Self-Regulatory Organizations (SROs).
The differences are of two sorts. One stems from obvious geographical
sources; American business is diverse, with ten local Stock Exchanges
(although that of New York with 82 per cent of the business is by far the
largest. UK activity is centred in London, with a single well-established
Stock Exchange, and the widest variety of other financial services. As a
result the SIB's task is both more concentrated and complex than that of
the SEC.

The other stems from differing political and social circumstances. The
SIB is not proposing to concern itself with the two most criticized activities –
takeovers and mergers, and the enforcement of insider dealing provisions,
both of which form an important part of the SEC's activities. Nor will it
have responsibility for public issues and listing, or the maintenance of
reporting standards. In the SIB's own words 'the focus is on the protection
of investors and the proper regulation and monitoring of intermediaries' –
the same priorities that had been underlined by the Gower and the Labour
Party reports. Quite, but is this enough? Over enthusiastic protection can
destroy markets as quickly as can fraud.

When the establishment of the SIB was first mooted the City was dubious:
anything it knew of the SEC it disliked and the SIB looked not dissimilar. City
institutions much preferred to be able to settle things among themselves, as
Lloyd's were doing, and in an attempt to retain the initiative the Governor
of the Bank of England appointed an advisory committee (in May 1984)
which was paralleled by a similar body in the Department of Trade,
which concerned itself with those aspects which were the Department's
responsibility.

As might have been expected the advisory committee suggested that,
rather than have an SEC-like body, government should formally delegate
to the City responsibility for organizing its own affairs through a private
agency. This constitutionally unprecedented solution was adopted by the
government in a White Paper and subsequently in the Financial Services
Bill.

The White Paper envisaged the SIB as being delegated powers from the
Department of Trade and Industry to monitor and regulate all business
concerned with the issue and sale of any form of securities and to delegate
in turn some of these powers to agencies formed by individual groups of
traders, of which the Stock Exchange was the most obvious if not the most
important. Established institutions might be very much left to their own
devices, having proved that these worked reasonably well, but new bodies
would face some strict requirements.

At first sight the SIB looked very much like another City triumph for
doing things its own way. The chairman of the SIB was to be appointed

by the Secretary of State with the approval of the Governor of the Bank of England; the members by the Governor with the agreement of the Secretary of State, a situation recalling the close domestic life of the Theban royal family. The powers delegated by the Secretary of State were wide, and placed the responsibility for control at a satisfactory distance from Parliament. John Plender and Paul Wallace, writing in 1984, could comment: 'At the end of the day, despite the rather chaotic nature of the proceedings, the Bank of England probably felt that it had some cause for satisfaction in the City Revolution ... it managed to set in train a reform of the City structure pretty much in its own terms.' The satisfaction may be shortlived, for as the Bill went through Parliament it became apparent that things were changing. It was inevitable that the left wing should press for sterner measures of control, and some of the arguments advanced were populist and confused. Dennis Skinner and Brian Sedgemore, self-appointed castigators of capitalism, were particularly long on indignation and short on information.

Not only Messrs Sedgemore and Skinner, but more experienced people like Anthony Nelson, Member for Chichester, were initiating moves to give the SIB statutory standing. In a debate in March 1986 Mr Nelson said that a wide range of powers to investigate and initiate prosecutions was denied to the SIB because of the impropriety of giving these powers to a private sector body. Speaking in the same debate Tim Smith, Member for Beaconsfield, suggested that a precedent for a statutory SIB could be the Audit Commission for England and Wales, established by the Department of the Environment in 1982 to scrutinize local government authorities. Providing its own finance by charging fees, the Audit Commission was not subject to Treasury controls on resources, in a fashion similar to that of the SEC.

As a result of the debate amendments were passed that gave the SIB powers to investigate the affairs of those outside the self-regulatory machine and to act as a prosecuting authority; these powers, if the SIB were to choose to exercise them, would extend its remit to cover such serious matters as insider trading, which it had until then excluded.

Some observers, indeed, believe that the SEC is already with us. *The Times*, commenting on the publication of the draft SIB rules, said:

One does not need to dwell long on the studied legalese of last week's weighty offerings from the Securities and Investments Board to reach an arresting conclusion; anybody in the futures business who fondly believed that London was not about to receive a Securities and Exchange Commission should think again.

Indeed the 'Conduct of Business Rules' issued by the SIB for consultation have quite unintentionally an almost Orwellian ring: 'deregulation' means exactly the opposite.

Under the guise of 'self-regulation' futures trading in London will in fact be carefully regulated by someone else ...

But the two crucial points remain. The SIB rules are comprehensive, and we are promised many more; and they are rules, not mere guidelines. Futures and options trading in London, for so long a world of its own, is moving into an uncomfortable era of direct and stringent controls.

By constructing the elaborate apparatus of SROs the Government has skilfully disguised the true extent of the central direction. Orwell would have understood.

The precise powers of the SIB may be of less importance than the character of those running it. In such ventures a firm beginning counts for more, as Joseph Kennedy proved at the SEC, David Lilienthal at the TVA, and Lord Shawcross at the Takeover Panel.

The first chairman of the SIB, Sir Kenneth Berrill, is a tough egg, with a wide experience of academic and public life, who threw himself into his task with energy. His initial views were against an SEC-like body, not from any tenderness towards wrongdoers, a subject on which he expresses himself vigorously, but for more pragmatic reasons.

His major objection being on the very grounds of effectiveness, in that were the SIB to be a statutory body it would negate the possibility of recruiting staff of a high enough calibre. In a lecture at Brunel University he said that he was

> not convinced that an effective regulatory body can be created wholly within the public sector, for the simple reason that public-sector financial and manning constraints will unavoidably, whatever promises and commitments may be given at the outset, limit the numbers and quality of staff that we can employ.

A complete answer to this should be that the Bank of England is a public-sector body, in fact a nationalized industry, yet manages to retain a free hand in the recruitment of staff – to pay, if necessary, well over the odds for the other nationalized industries. We have seen, however, that the Bank of England has had to fight for its continued privileged existence, which it has justified by performance. Starting a new body is a horse of a very different colour, especially with the record of consistent political interference in commercial matters. Even the well-established SEC is now being forced by US budget restrictions to cut back on its activities.

Estimating the likely course of events in the near future it would seem that the stronger the powers of the SIB, the better. For anyone who experienced the boom and crash of the early 1970s it is not too difficult to forecast the short-term effect of present movements, and the problems these will present to the regulatory authorities. In an expanding market traders will find it easy to make profits; everything they touch seems to turn to gold. When markets stagnate, and begin to reverse, as inevitably they do, life becomes more difficult.

Dealers are inspired by results; their personal profits, while welcome, are only part of the story. Recent years have given many examples of dealers falsifying returns in order to make their results seem better, even when there was no question of direct financial benefit to them; on the contrary, they were well aware of the inevitable consequences when discovered. If the added spur of immense personal gain is added, then the temptation to cook the books will in some cases become irresistible. A cautionary tale of what can happen, even in the tightly regulated American market, and even in the largest firms, is provided by the story of Leslie Roberts, arrested by the FBI in February 1985 in connection with a fraud involving some $9 million from a New York broker.

Newspaper reports allege that having failed in the University of Miami a couple of times Mr Roberts was, not unnaturally, in 1983, at the ripe age of twenty, recruited by Interwest, a now defunct broker. Mr Roberts served and worked in Miami; the broker's head office was in Colorado. One of his colleagues reported: 'Everything is done by telephone. Leslie was a natural. He was very good on the phone. He had a great phone personality, and he was very, very, hungry for success.' He certainly succeeded in making money for himself, earning as much as $26,000 on commission in a single transaction.

Mr Roberts's activity became known at the centre of things by one of the largest and most respectable New York brokers, who enticed him away from Interwest to their own Miami office. By that time Mr Roberts was claiming to be a graduate of his university; a claim that was never checked. It was not only Mr Roberts's personal abilities that made him a desirable property, but the fact that he had a rich uncle, a Mr Frank Gory, who was prepared to entrust his not insubstantial fortune, some $17 million, to Mr Roberts.

Even for one of his reputed ability the rewards of Mr Roberts's success were striking – two chauffeur-driven limousines on 24-hour notice, an executive jet, and a $1.6 million house; he claimed to be making a quarter of a million dollars a month for himself and as much or more for his employers.

Anxious to acquire the services of this golden boy, a competing big New York-based firm – lured him to their own Miami office.

To any employer less optimistic such sums as Mr Roberts claimed to earn might have caused raised eyebrows. Brokers acting for individuals make their money by levying commissions on each transaction at a reducing percentage: on smaller accounts there may be a fixed minimum per annum charge. Since the more transactions that are put through an account, the greater the broker's income, the temptation to maximize activity is obvious, but usually held in check by a broker's own honesty and discretion. Every client receives regular valuations of his portfolio, and if these show better than average growth he will not be likely to object to a number of ins and outs, especially if these produce capital gains rather than income. But if the account is hyperactive, and still does worse, or even loses, then the client will feel aggrieved and make highly audible complaints.

On a large account such as Mr Gory's, broking commissions charged on transactions which would be expected to be individually substantial and would not be expected to exceed one half per cent; if the portfolio were turned over once a year this would yield a profit to the broking firm of $85,000. And once a year would be pretty active; a well-balanced portfolio should contain long-term growth stocks which might be expected to be held for years. Four times a year, which would involve buying and selling all the stocks once every three months, would be very odd indeed, but would still only produce some $340,000, of which at most one third might be split with the dealer, giving him commissions of about $115,000 a year; Mr Roberts is said to have claimed twice that amount a *month*.

Very shortly after Mr Roberts left, his first New York employers discovered that Mr Gory's portfolio had been moved in a frenzy of activity that had indeed resulted in these astounding levels of commission, but at the cost of depleting the capital value from $17 million to $8.2 million. Mr Roberts had it seemed collected some $2.4 million in commissions in two years, allegedly avoiding any inconvenient family disputes, always unpleasant, by the simple stratagem of submitting an entirely fictitious set of accounts and reports to his uncle.

It was in this that Mr Roberts's alleged crime lay: hyperactivity on a customer's account, popularly known as 'churning', is a matter of degree. There are clients who encourage frequent movements in their portfolios, just as there are those who have sacred cows, such as Aunt Agatha's War Loan, that they refuse to have disturbed: a sharp manager can often do better for the first group, and make himself much more commission income in the process, than one who is restricted, or restricts himself, to a limited number of transactions. The allegations in these reports are disputed by Mr Roberts, and his lawyers have stated in defense that, when all the evidence is out, it will be apparent that he had full discretion to trade and was sincerely attempting to make Mr Gory money.

The SIB's draft rule on the subject underlined the difficulty, saying only, in effect, that churners knew when they were doing it, and that they shouldn't.

Under the traditional Stock Exchange system one trusts that Mr Roberts would have had a less easy time. Any stockbroker would wish more knowledge of an applicant's background; supervision would have been constant; several years would be required before he was allowed to operate on discretion; commissions of such magnitude would never have been paid, such flamboyant living would very quickly have come to the partners' attention, and most significantly he would not have been operating 1500 miles from his head office.

Much of this will soon be radically changed. Under the new rules of ownership a portfolio of the size of Mr Gory's might be handled, not by the investment management department of an accepting house responsible to the Bank of England, nor a firm of stockbrokers in the closed community of the Exchange, but by one of the new conglomerates, staffed by people from different backgrounds, newly come together, operating several stops away on the underground, and subject to much less close supervision than has been usual.

In such a financial conglomerate Mr Gory's portfolio might well be diversified from Stock Exchange quoted securities into international equities, Euronotes, commercial paper, financial futures, and over-the-counter markets. The supervision of these markets falls outside the Stock Exchange's remit, and would be the concern of another self-regulatory authority such as ISRO (International Securities Regulatory Organization) or AFBD (Association of Future Brokers and Dealers).

Supposing Mr Gory were to be a client of the division of a banking group which also handled new issues and merger business. The doctrine is that an unbreakable 'Chinese Wall' exists between the two activities; the executives, should they meet, confine the conversation to the weather: business must never be mentioned lest a hint might be dropped that would have the effect of improperly enriching – *horribile dictu* – the staff or clients of the investment division.

It is possible to believe in such exalted restraint in the old acccepting houses. From my own experience I can guarantee that it existed in William Brandt's, where portfolio management staff led an entirely independent existence. With highly paid dealers operating in new organizations without corporate traditions, striving to keep up their excessive earnings, on the qui vive for anything that may help them to do so, it becomes difficult not to suspect at least a chink or two in the Chinese Wall. It becomes impossible when the existence of widespread organized irregularities is common knowledge.

The Stock Exchange surveillance department, for example, is convinced that organized rings in several City institutions have been making use of forward knowledge of impending takeovers to buy shares and deal on a large scale through their own off-shore companies. Michael Feltham, a member of that department, was reported as saying: 'Time and time again our investigations have run up against a brick wall of an off-shore company whose true ownership we cannot discover.' Fifty of the 284 investigations made by the Stock Exchange since 1980, when insider dealing was made a criminal offence, have been frustrated by such tactics.

With the accent on performance the pressure will be greater to increase commissions, and the temptations to cheat more numerous. The dealer's manager will be on commission, and the director in charge will probably have a share in the profits. They in turn will report, probably indirectly, to bank directors to whom the whole business is unexplored territory.

If things go wrong not only will the Bank of England want to investigate improper trading in a bank department, but the Stock Exchange or other agency and the SIB will have responsibility for the dealing activities, the relevant Ombudsman will be ready to take up the cudgels on behalf of the aggrieved investor, and the DPP will be waiting for someone to tell him, please, what is going on.

PART SEVEN
Uneasy City

Uneasy City

'But, these same citizens, they are such sharks.'

BEN JOHNSON

The City has moved in the last quarter century from being the centre of a crumbling Empire, servicing a rapidly disappearing sterling area and declining domestic industry, to being an international marketplace. In some aspects it was already so: Lloyd's, the Baltic and Commodity Exchanges were international. They have become, especially Lloyd's, more so, and the domestic market has shrunk, and expansion has perforce been into international business institutions. The change has come most notably in banking; British banks now have over half their assets in currencies other than sterling.

As a result the City has escaped the fate of other British industries and has flourished even more than it did at the height of imperial prosperity. It has not succeeded without distorting the economy and society. Eggs, financial and human, have been loaded into its capacious basket.

One of the more horrifying spectacles of 1986 was a full-page advertisement placed in the newspapers by a well-known firm of accountants that revealed that 10 per cent of all young people graduating in 1985 had applied to join that one firm. Similarly large numbers presumably applied to other firms of accountants. That so many of our brightest young people (and, according to the Cambridge University Appointments Board, many of them among the more academically successful) can seek no finer end than to be bookkeepers is disturbing enough, but the consequences are even more so.

The role of the accountant in industry is admittedly always necessary and sometimes important, but it is essentially negative. Companies may avoid bankruptcy by the skill of their accountants, but they do not become successful thereby. It is the engineers, the scientists, and the salesmen who generate growth. In the special context of financial services the position changes; the figures men are also the production engineers and researchers: it is their talents that create new products and profits.

So far they have been successful, and the City has flourished, but both the costs and the risks must be noted. The costs are those of taking so much of the national talent. Jobs in merchant and investment banks, stockbrokers, and accountants are sought after to the virtual exclusion of industry, commerce and public service. Oxbridge remains nearly as successful in obtaining the plums for its graduates as it did when those plums were of a different flavour. Top City positions are shared now just about equally between Oxford, Cambridge and the others. The cultural gap between City and the rest of Britain shows no sign of further narrowing.

The risks are those of catastrophic failure, and the effectiveness of the regulatory authorities in monitoring trading therefore a matter of prime concern.

In order to be useful and effectual rules must be accepted by the generality of society. If too many of the populace drive motor vehicles at excessive speeds or smoke illicit herbal mixtures one cannot expect the laws that prohibit such action to be vigorously enforced. Indeed, if rules are widely disobeyed the utility of the rule itself must be questioned.

It would be a frustrating waste of energy therefore to burden financial institutions with regulations that too many practitioners refuse to abide by. If this point of view is accepted the merit of self-regulation becomes obvious. The Kennel Club and breed associations contrive, not without effort, to secure adhesion to their decrees since these are accepted as reasonable and to the benefit of doggery: a pitifully small percentage of dog licences were ever applied for, since these were seen to be footling. Golf club rules are followed a good deal more closely than those in prisons, in spite of the usually stricter discipline in force in the latter institutions.

This argument has had a good deal of force: few people have been cheated by building societies; banks may make errors but are usually more than willing to correct them; stockbrokers rarely defraud their clients, and are quickly dealt with if they do, and no policy holder at Lloyd's has ever suffered by the defalcation of underwriters. Compared with any other financial centre London is a rosebed. Or has been, since there are ominous signs that things are changing.

With the passing of stiff collars and umbrellas some of the virtue has gone, and cannot be recalled. Moral suasion, which was effective when the Bank of England could rely upon the Discount Houses Association and the Accepting Houses Committee to rally their numbers, has had to be replaced by a battery of controls operated by a greatly increased staff. It is tempting to be a *laudator temporis acti*, in the spirit of Mary Whitehouse, and attribute changes to a decline from the standards of morality observed in one's own youth. People have been doing this for several thousand years, with impressive continuity, and thereby prove their folly.

More stringent controls are vital, not because of any growth in commercial depravity, but because altered conditions demand them. Prophecy can be a risky business, but in financial matters it is safe to emulate Jeremiah: disasters can always be relied upon to happen. It is beyond doubt that in the next few years there will be an international financial crisis, fraudulent brokerage dealings, and false insurance claims. What decade, if not lustre, has been without them? Financial difficulties have the most respectable antiquity; the case against Dionysodorus advanced by Demosthenes could be paralleled today in any commercial court.

What differentiates the coming stormclouds from the past is their size and international complexity. Banks, which twenty years ago had most of their assets in their domestic currency, now have a wide spread. The most important international currency is the US dollar, which has shown itself to be highly volatile (in the 12 months April 1985–86 the dollar underwent fluctuations of up to 50 per cent against sterling, and similar ranges against other major currencies).

The nature of assets has become more uncertain. A bill of exchange, a term loan, or an overdraft are clearly definable and well understood, but the ever-proliferating variety of Euro-instruments are neither. The liabilities of banks in the new securitization of debt have yet to be established. In spite of the efforts of the central bankers no firm agreement on the co-ordination of bank supervision has been reached. Widely differing interpretations of the valuation of assets are found between such well-controlled centres as London and New York (the valuation of Crocker under British standards was 25 per cent higher than that required by the American authorities).

Loopholes always remain. The Bank of England and the Federal Reserve may be thorough in everything they do; the Basle committee moves towards regulating international instruments, but the whole Euronote market remains footloose, finding homes wherever these may seem most profitable. These are often where controls are least stringent: the popularity of Liechtenstein owes little to its scenery, and Tristan da Cunha is becoming a centre for ship operators not because of its geographical convenience.

An added dimension of risk is that brought by increasingly sophisticated data transmission. An old-fashioned balance sheet fraud is shown up on an audit and responsibility can be pinned down. Computer-based fraud is quicker to perpetrate and much more difficult to trace; the proceeds can be siphoned off into a secret account with equal facility. In the absence of effective international monitoring such refuges will continue to be available and secure.

To anticipate risks is not necessarily to avoid them, and the authorities responsible for doing so find themselves in very different states of preparation. The Bank of England is better equipped than ever to fight the last war, and is keenly conscious of the dangers that may be encountered in the next. Its powers, although great, are limited. In the councils of the central banks, as exemplified by the Basle committee, the Bank is *primus inter pares*, and exerts great moral authority, now bent on securing some form of international control. Although progress has been made, effective agreement is not yet achieved, and it will probably take an international banking crisis to stimulate unanimous action.

At home the bank can seek but to influence governments. It has done so successfully in the projected legislation but faces greater challenges. In order to achieve a solution to Third–World debts a programme agreed by the developed countries is needed. Any such programme must include official support, either to creditor banks or to debtor governments, which runs clean counter to the prejudices of the UK and USA administrations. Mr James Baker (US Treasury Secretary) has pushed out the boat, and there is little sign of a crew clambering aboard.

Once again, such action will probably need a disaster to trigger it, and the only sure thing about disasters is their inevitability.

In more domestic matters, Lloyd's is best left alone to work out its own salvation in tears of repentance. Lloyd's names certainly need protecting against fraud by those who act on their behalf, and the council is seized of the need to do so, but the question of regulation at Lloyd's deserves a better understanding. There are only two classes of people likely to suffer there from fraud: policy holders and names. Policy holders may be the victims of dishonest brokers, but Lloyd's represents only a single outlet. When fraud has been practised in the past it has been outside Lloyd's, as with the infamous Emil Savundra. Lloyd's have a comprehensive arrangement of their own for reimbursement, and Lloyd's policy holders are well protected.

Malpractice may be – as in some recent cases – against the names themselves. These are, or should be, a sophisticated group. They are advised in some detail of their responsibilities; they are given full details of the past performance of the syndicates they may wish to join, and indeed of any others that they may wish to see. The committee goes to some lengths, in a personal interview, to ensure that all this is fully comprehended.

The Council has already admitted the principle of needing to compensate names who have suffered by criminal acts on the part of their managing agents: the border between criminality and negligence, and the question of negligence, needs definition, and the machinery for compensation formalizing; but the principle is there.

As an active pressure group, the Association of Lloyd's Names, is keeping a beady eye on their interests, and it is unlikely that anything too injurious will now get past them.

Building societies are another matter. The race for the high-street business is now on, and building societies, once they get their Act together, are anxious to compete with each other, with the clearing banks, TSB, National Giro, mortgage houses, insurance brokers, and come who may. In the contest the cosy image of building societies is unlikely to last, except perhaps as a relic of former times among a few surviving small and local institutions. Big societies will exercise their new found freedom to diversify; the first-mortgage-to-newly-weds, which has done so much to contribute to their present character, will continue to decline in importance. Smaller societies, wishing to emulate, will be forced into mergers.

Secondary mortgage trading, already common in the US but only now beginning in the UK, will reinforce these changes. This process, whereby primary lending institutions sell packages of mortgages to investors, destroys the intimate relationship between borrower and lender, and forces institutions into inflexible policies. Some adventurous societies will take things at too smart a pace and, having neither depth of management or experience in lending, will come a cropper. The solidity of the business, with the reluctance of the house owner to jeopardize possession of his home underpinning the paradoxical success of the borrowing-short and lending-long practice, will be further undermined by the change in family patterns. An increasing proportion of householders are single-parent families and single people, whose finances tend to be more precarious than those of the traditional multi-breadwinner household. Since 1980 the number of properties repossessed by societies has quadrupled; at least 100,000 borrowers are currently experiencing repayment difficulties.

Given the paucity of qualified staff experienced in the new business that the societies want to try, casualties will be inevitable. The task of sorting these out will fall to the new regulatory organization, the Building Societies Commission. This will not be one of Sir Kenneth Berrill's SROs, nor responsible to the Bank of England, but a non-ministerial government department, subject to Treasury control, and therefore auguring poorly for its prospects in competing with the SROs for staff. The first commissioner will appropriately be the present Chief Registrar of Friendly Societies, Michael Bridgeman.

Altogether the most entertaining spectacle of the post-Big Bang world will be observing the SROs getting down to the business of restraining the more adventurous members of their communities. There are not many of them, but among them are those who combined to make the British Telecom issue the most flagrant and widely dispersed case of its kind in modern times. The Stock Exchange investigations team duly investigated, and by early 1986 four stockbrokers, four company directors and one lawyer had received summonses in what was hoped would be the first case. Should this be successful, I was assured by the Stock Exchange supervisors, many more would follow. Lord Hailsham, commenting on the matter in October 1985, gave some flavour of the urgency with which the matter was pressed.

> A large number of applications were received. What had to be done was to enquire of the banks as to the analysis of the applications that they had received and for the banks to pool their information, then for those to whom the inquiry was delegated to see whether there appeared any traces of impropriety.
>
> That has now been done and the law officers will no doubt come to their decision in due course . . .

The law's delays have not much improved since the Prince of Denmark's complaint.

The danger of confusion was recognized by the sib in its 1985 paper 'The Regulation of Investment Business':

> Because membership of an sro will not necessarily permit a firm to do all types of investment business, a number of firms will need to join more than one sro in order to do a full range of business. It is even possible that some may be authorized by sro membership for some functions and by direct authorization for others. It is also likely that within many financial groups there will be subsidiaries authorized by a range of sros. The Board is concerned to minimize the complexity and inconvenience that may result from such multiple authorization. Problems of this sort are most likely to rise in the context of financial surveillance – that is, setting and monitoring compliance with liquid capital and similar rules – and the Board proposes to introduce a lead regulator policy to ensure that responsibilities in the area (and in the area alone) are clearly allocated to a single authority.
>
> The lead regulator will generally be the sro responsible for the largest part of a firm's business. Other sros will be able to provide for financial monitoring of the firm to be done by the sro which is lead regulator; for each multiple-authorized form there will need to be a clear understanding as to which sro this will be, and the Board will wish to be informed of all such arrangements.

Well, there will, indeed there will, have to be a clear understanding. But unless the sro and the Board are able to cope with crisis management even this modest degree of clarity will not be enough. A permanent staff of experienced professionals is essential, and they are going to be difficult to come by, since the liveliest talents will find the prospects of poaching more exciting than those of gamekeeping, at least until a bear market sets in.

Ultimately, it has to be the banks who take the strain, and face the task, with or without the assistance of the Bank of England and government. How well able they are to do so will depend on their ability to strengthen their balance sheets and the success with which these recover from the international debt and energy crises. It is certain that some will do so less well than others.

Even the best of balance sheets will avail little unless the banks fulfil the hopes that the Bank of England has expressed and ensure that they have boards capable of directing increasingly large and complex enterprises honestly and prudently.

Bibliography

Attali, J., *A Man of Influence*, London 1986
Chester, N., *The Nationalisation of British Industry*, London 1975
Clapham, J., *The Bank of England: A History*, Cambridge 1944
Clarke, W.M., *Inside the City*, London 1983
Cripps, F. et. al., *Manifesto*, London 1981
Davis, S.I., *The Euro-Bank*, London 1980
Department of Trade and Industry Report on Pergamon Ltd, 1974
Dictionary of National Biography
Economist Special Report 222, *All Change in the City*, Nick Hewlett & Jan
   Toporowski
Ferris, P., *The City*, London 1960
Gower, L., *Report on Investor Protection*, London 1984
Hanson, P.G., *Service Banking*, London 1982
Heller, R. & Willatt N., *Can You Trust Your Bank?* London 1977
Hodgson, G., *Lloyd's of London*, London 1984
Institute of Bankers, *Banks and the Public*, London 1981
Kindleberger, C.P., *Manias, Panics and Crashes*, London 1978
Labour Party Study Group on the City: Report, London 1982
Lever, H. & Huhne, C., *Debt and Danger*, London 1985
Mace, M., *Directors – Myth and Reality*, Harvard 1985
McRae, H. & Cairncross, F., *Capital City*, London 1973
Minns, R., *Take over the City*, London 1982
Moran, M., *The Politics of Banking* 1984
Plender, J. & Wallace P., *The Square Mile*, London 1985
Reid, M., *The Secondary Banking Crisis*, London 1982
Revell, J., *The British Financial System*, London 1973
Sampson, A., *The Changing Anatomy of Britain*, London 1982
Sayers, R.S., *The Bank of England 1891–1944*, Cambridge 1976
Sayers, R.S., (ed) *Banking in Western Europe*, Oxford 1972
Taylor, A.J.P., *England 1914–45*, Oxford 1972
Thirsk, J. & Cooper, J.P., *Seventeenth Century Economic Development*, Oxford
   1972
Weschsberg, J., *The Merchant Bankers*, London 1970

Periodicals
Brookings Institute: Papers on Economic Activity
Bank of England: Quarterly Review
National Westminster Bank: Quarterly Review
Barclays Bank Review

Index

Page references in italic indicate Tables.